SpringerBriefs in Law

More information about this series at http://www.springer.com/series/10164

Elina Moustaira

Art Collections, Private and Public: A Comparative Legal Study

Springer

Elina Moustaira
Faculty of Law
University of Athens
Athens
Greece

ISSN 2192-855X ISSN 2192-8568 (electronic)
SpringerBriefs in Law
ISBN 978-3-319-15801-3 ISBN 978-3-319-15802-0 (eBook)
DOI 10.1007/978-3-319-15802-0

Library of Congress Control Number: 2015932066

Springer Cham Heidelberg New York Dordrecht London

Printed on acid-free paper

Springer International Publishing AG Switzerland is part of Springer Science+Business Media (www.springer.com)

Preface

In our times art is often created in order to constitute a part of a collection, private or public. It is not anymore conceived as part of a temple, a church, or a royal palace, as it was in the far past, but on the contrary it is destined to the isolated space of public or private collections. According to a certain opinion, this fact strengthened the oecumenical dimension of the art.

Art collections, as everything that concerns artworks, cultural objects in general, need an interdisciplinary approach, even when one wants to study their legal treatment.

A basic difference between the private and the public collections is that the latter are most often inalienable. Because of that, it is not easy to correct a "mistake" or, in other words, this is the reason why the "right to the mistake" is decisive in the history of art.

Notwithstanding their difference(s), the connection between public museums and private collections is very close: On the one hand, public museums, especially of contemporary art, may have a strong influence on the choices of artworks by private collectors and on the other hand, many museums were based on private collections or/and accept donations of artworks by private collectors.

Uses and legal regulations were and are often copied by states. Therefore, museums—a Western concept—were and are created all over the world, but also private collections are created and grow in various states, not only Western.

Copying laws is not a guarantee for a uniform legal treatment and is not always successful. Details in the legal mentality, the legal culture of each state cause differences at the interpretation or/and the application of laws. It follows from this that there are many—sometimes enormous—differences in the various laws as far as the constitution, management, etc., of private collections and (public) museums are concerned.

For example: There are different models of cultural politics that the states follow, with the (one of more) obvious consequence of difference in the treatment of public and private art collections. Sometimes collectors' rights are "confronted" with the artists' rights. The differences in national laws as far as this "confrontation" is concerned, are often big.

The circulation of the artworks may have unforeseen and undesirable results if it is not controlled. Different states have different legal regulations. These differences are due to various factors which may be taken into account by the states' legislators. However, it seems that there is a general agreement that the documentation of the artworks' provenance is very important. "All the countries should have or try to create systems that would prevent suspect or clearly illicit acquisitions of artworks."

Obviously, a complete study of all these issues would need several volumes; such is the richness and the complexity of the legal regulations enforced by the various states. Nevertheless, I tried to present as clearly as I could the legal "landscape" of the art collections, public and private, using detailed examples of the legal treatment of different issues by the national laws.

I would like to thank Springer-Verlag GmbH and especially Dr. Brigitte Reschke, Springer Executive Editor Law, for her precious advices.

Contents

Chapter 1
Introduction: Collecting Art

1.1 General Comments

Studying and writing about the legal regulation of art collections is a really very interesting and not at all easy or simple work. It absolutely needs an inter- or multidisciplinary approach. Law, of course, but also art history, sociology, and economy are intervening. A perfect field for comparative law research, that is!

The word's origin is the Latin term "collectio", derivative of the verb "colligere"—the latter comes from the verb "légere" which has its origin in the Greek verb "λέγειν".

What is art?[1] What is an artwork? Which is the essence of an art collection? When does a compilation of artworks may be called an art collection? Which are the distinctive aspects of such an art collection?

Collecting art works has been one of the central axes on which art history has been based. One could speak about history of collectors—and, according to a point of view, of the patrons with whom collectors were somehow related.

Collecting art is a cryptic world, they say, inherent perhaps in the human instinct of gathering objects. Collecting art sometimes covers complicated and changing realities. It often served to save cultural heritage of peoples and it fed public collections. Collecting art, they say, reflects the sensibility of the society in front of the artistic fact.[2]

Collecting art has not only positive aspects. Negative rumors also circulate about it. It is accused, sometimes rightly sometimes wrongly, for being a crucial factor of illicit excavations and illicit trade.

Collecting creates new identities, both of the object collected and of the collector, it is argued.[3]

---

[1] "This is one of the great, sticky questions of the past hundred years", McIver Lopes 2014, p. 1.
[2] Galván Romarate-Zabala 1997, pp. 11–12.
[3] Van der Grijp 2006, p. 12.

E. Moustaira, *Art Collections, Private and Public: A Comparative Legal Study*,
SpringerBriefs in Law, DOI 10.1007/978-3-319-15802-0_1

Collecting is a "thoroughly creative work, not primarily a question of managing and conserving which many people tend to think", as is declared.[4] And so it is. Still, besides categorization and organization, management and conservation of collected objects are very important for the duration of the collections, private or public.

1.2 What Is Art? What Is an Art Work?

As it is argued in recent treatises, the question "what is art" is answered by theories of art which state what it is for an object to be a work of art.[5]

Art is not a "natural" kind,[6] it is something that we, the human beings have created.[7] Philosophers trying to give a definition of art, proceed to a conceptual analysis. So we try to understand the conceptual sketch of some probably not durable human practice. Human practices, as social inventions, are stable in a given time and place, they change over time, they change from culture to culture and they are often based on our biological characteristics and on our common experience.[8]

Is there a definition that could be applied in all cultures and at all times? "Fine art" is a concept that was essentially born during the Age of Enlightenment. The modern concept of art was born from this idea of the "fine art", according to an opinion. Consequently, it is a relatively recent invention, localized in a specific social and cultural space, the so called Western one. There, the art is conceptually distinct from the practical everyday aspects of life. On the contrary, in the frame of most if not all traditional native cultures, "art" may be connected to theology, to the various cultural world views[9] as well as to the crystallization of these views in government institutions, in law, and in material aspects of the everyday life.[10]

---

[4] Svanberg 2008, p. 175.

[5] McIver Lopes 2014, p. 11.

[6] See McIver Lopes 2014, writing about "Theories and Concepts of Art" and commenting on Hillary Putnam's showing that, "for some kinds, having a concept of the kind is consistent with considerable ignorance about the nature of the kind", p. 69: "It does not follow from this that art is a natural kind. Probably it is not, if there would be no works of art without agents who respond to them in certain ways. However, the choice is not to find the nature of art either to be implicit in the folk concept of art or in a concept of art that figures in the hypotheses and explanations of the natural sciences. That is a false dichotomy because the natural sciences do not have a monopoly on empirical inquiry.

[7] Moustaira 2012, p. 28.

[8] Clowney 2011, p. 311.

[9] See Moustakas 1989, pp. 1195–1196: "art links group members to their ancestors and heirs, thereby both satisfying a basic need for identity and symbolizing shared values".

[10] Tsosie 2009, p. 5.

Being more extreme, not inaccurate though, one could argue that artworks have lives and their lives depend on the context and the circumstances in which they are led.[11]

Given this fact, it does not seem possible to have a general definition of art. Art, it is argued, is always based on cultural and social practices. The art work is the product of various "meetings": meetings of ideas, of persons, of ways of thinking, of techniques, of stories. And all these meetings could be gathered in one and only creation or they could give meaning to all the works of an artist.[12]

1.3 The Importance of Cultural Property

It is with a splendid description that a Spanish scholar presents this at first sight curious phenomenon: in our times, when one speaks so much about globalization, the "local" has become very important.

As he points out, although they seem as the two opposites of one reality, one could think of them as the essential variables of an equation. Thus, more and more think that parallel to the increasing phenomenon of the globalization the local reality becomes evident, a reality which is expression of a powerful collective identity and of potential strategies of development. In this line of thought, the globalization would not have any sense or it would have poor sense, if it were not seated on local realities that nutrition the global phenomenon.[13]

Cultural property, cultural heritage, in the Western world at first had almost the same meaning as art[14]; culture was the "high culture", the "opera-house" definition of it.[15]

The terms acquired a broader content mainly at the time International Conventions on relative issues started being discussed and adopted.

As far as issues about preservation of cultural objects are concerned, it was after the World War I that they began to receive more attention.[16] In 1931, at the International Conference for the Protection and Conservation of Artistic and Historical Monuments, the Athens Charter was agreed,[17] focusing on the safeguard of historic cities. Article 8 of the Charter states: "Items of sculpture, painting or

---

[11] See Carrier 2006, p. 4: "In an Indian temple a sculpture is worshipped. Transported to an American museum, that artifact becomes art. And so a theory is required to explain how an object can survive such dramatic changes. To learn what it is to lead the life of a work of art, we need to understand museums".

[12] Somé 2007, p. 15.

[13] Gómez Pellón 2011, p. 67.

[14] "Art as the predominant genre of cultural property", see Moustakas 1989, p. 1195.

[15] Said 1993, pp. xii–xiv.

[16] Scott 2013, p. 53.

[17] Iamandi 1997, p. 17.

decoration which form an integral part of a monument may only be removed from it if this is the sole means of ensuring their preservation".

The World War II and the destructions it caused "led" to the 1954 Hague Convention for the Protection of Cultural Property in the Event of Armed Conflict and its First Protocol. A Second Protocol to this Convention was adopted in 1999.

Probably the two more important International Conventions on cultural property issues, as far as the effects they have, are the 1970 UNESCO Convention on the Means of Prohibiting and Preventing the Illicit Import, Export, and Transfer of Ownership of Cultural Property and the 1995 UNIDROIT Convention on Stolen or Illegally Exported Cultural Objects

The discussions about many issues concerning culture,[18] cultural heritage, cultural property, cultural patrimony,[19] are still heated and different arguments are presented by jurists of the various countries, of the various legal systems. While others insist that there are differences between the terms cultural heritage[20] and cultural property, reflecting different mentalities,[21] others state that these terms have no specific meaning and may both include "human artifacts as well as natural objects or places".[22]

Still, there is difference between the terms, but they are often used interchangeably.

Undoubtedly, both the universalist approach and the nationalist approach to the term cultural property implicate groups, values, collective production and collective meaning.[23]

1.4 Are Definitions Important?

In many if not most national laws there are no legislative definitions either of the artwork or of the private collections or of the museums. There is no certainty whatever, as far as those concepts are concerned. Especially for the museums, this is brilliantly described by *Karsten Schubert*:

> The museum is changing. In the past it was a place of absolute certainties, the fount of definitions, values and education in all matters artistic, a place not of questions but of authoritative answers. Today, the museum is at the center of a heated debate about its nature

[18] Moustaira 2006, pp. 20–21.

[19] In 1959, André Malreaux wrote about cultural patrimony (*patrimoine culture*).

[20] See Nafziger and Paterson 2014a, p. 1: "Broadly speaking, the term "cultural heritage" refers to the myriad manifestations of culture that human beings have inherited from their forebears. These manifestations include, for example: art, architecture, rural and urban landscapes, crafts, music, language, literature, film, documentary and digital records, folklore and oral history, culinary traditions, indigenous medicine, ceremonies and rituals, religion, sports and games, dance and other performing arts, and recreational practices such as those involving hunting and fishing".

[21] See Nafziger and Paterson 2014b, p. 29: "Generally, the concept of cultural patrimony leads to sovereign ownership or more limited regulatory authority over both public and private material".

[22] Sax 1990, p. 1142.

[23] Mezey 2007, pp. 2010–2011.

> and methodology. At the most extreme, the museum's very purpose is questioned – and denied. It is a perpetually inconclusive discussion, yet it profoundly affects the way museums are perceived and run.[24]

A rather rare exception to the absence of legislative definitions of the museums, is Portuguese law according to which the museum is "an institution of permanent character, with or without legal personality, non-profit, endowed with an organizational structure that allows it to: (a) Ensure a unitary destination to a set of cultural assets and value them through research, incorporation, inventory, documentation, conservation, interpretation, exhibition and publicizing, with scientific, educational and recreational aims; (b) provide regular access to the public and foster the democratization of culture, the promotion of person and the development of Society" (Article 3, para 1, Museums Act).

As it is stated,[25] the Portuguese legal museum's concept seems to have been inspired by the Code of Ethics for Museums, of the International Council of Museums (ICOM),[26] according to which, the museum is a "non-profit" making permanent institution in the service of society and of its development, open to the public, which acquires, conserves, researches, communicates and exhibits, for purposes of study, education and enjoyment, the tangible and intangible evidence of people and their environment".

In France too, the Museums' Law (*loi relative aux musées de France*) of 4.1.2001, contains a juridical definition of museum.

"The museums are worlds", says poetically *J.M.G. Le Clézio*, mentioning at the same time that they are the result of conquests, of plunders, of legs, of exchanges.[27]

In Italian law there is no legislative definition of the artwork. On the contrary, there is a legislative definition of cultural object (*bene culturale*) in the Article 10, c. 1 of the *Codice dei Beni Culturali*—a definition absolutely bureaucratic, as it is stated: "Cultural goods are the movable and immovable objects that belong to the State, to the regions, to other territorial public entities, as well as to every other public entity and institute and to private non-profit legal persons, which present an artistic, historical, archaeological or ethno-anthropological interest".[28]

---

[24] Schubert 2009, p. 15.

[25] Laureano 2014, p. 10.

[26] ICOM was created in 1946. It is a non-governmental organization and the only organization in the world, of museums and museum professionals committed to the promotion and protection of tangible and intangible cultural heritage.

[27] "Les musées sont des mondes, n'en doutons pas. Nés du hasard ou, si le mot effraie, forgés comme nous-mêmes dans la fantaisie. Objets flottants, réunis par la vague et poussés par le flux sur le rivage, au gré des conquêtes, des pillages, des legs et des échanges. … Les mondes dont ils proviennent, où sont-ils? Oubliés, effacés, revenus à la poussière, avec les mains, les yeux, les visages qui les ont créés.", Le Clézio 2011, p. 15.

[28] "Sono beni culturali le cose immobili e mobili appartenenti allo Stato, alle regioni, agli altri enti pubblici territoriai, nonché da ogni altro ente ed istituto pubblico e a persone giuridiche private senza fine di lucro, che presentano interesse artistico, storico, archeologico o etnoantropologico".

According to one opinion, the existence of this legislative (bureaucratic) definition obliges the legislator to stabilize a mechanism via which an object is recognized as cultural object (Articles 12, 13 and 14 of the Code) and at the same time to make lists of possible categories of cultural objects (Articles 10 and 11), something that entails the danger to exclude certain objects or to wait some years until the object can "enter into the big family of cultural goods".[29]

However, Italian law is one of the few who have a definition of the museum. Thus, the *Codice dei Beni Culturali* defines the museums as a "permanent structure which acquires, conserves, orders and exhibits cultural objects with the aim of education and study" (Article 101, c. 2a).[30]

It is argued that the fact that in most national laws there are no normative definitions has consequences on the production of the necessary documents that rule the art transactions, national and international, creating perplexity and uncertainty.[31] On the other hand, there are those who oppose to the above complaint that art transactions are almost everywhere notable for their relative informality.

1.5 Identity of Collectors

Every object has two functions, it is stated: we can use it and we can appropriate it. These two functions are mutually exclusive. When an object stops being defined on the basis of its practical utility, it acquires exclusively subjective value: its fate is to become a collection's object.[32]

What does this need of accumulating parts of an aimed whole reveals[33]?

According to an opinion, not far from the truth for certain time periods and for certain people, collecting is a way for the rich people to pass their time. According to this opinion, collection means accumulating unnecessary objects and through this, provocatively showing off to the others that some people can dispose freely their time as well as the "material translation" of this time too.[34]

According to another opinion, someone who has too much money is a bad collector, since this economic wellbeing facilitates exorbitantly the acquisition of art works therefore the pleasure of hunting is lost. The collector, it is stated, has "the olfaction of a hunter, the soul of a policeman, the objectivity of a historian, the prudence of a horse merchant"[35]! Often, though, as it is pointed out, the collector is

---

[29] Pinna 2005, p. 48 and n. 9.

[30] "struttura permanente che acquisisce, conserva, ordina ed espone beni culturali per finalita di educazione e di studio".

[31] Sandretto Re Rebaudengo 2011, pp. 90–91.

[32] Baudrillard 1994, p. 8.

[33] Moustaira 2012, p. 54.

[34] Attali 1997, p. 19.

[35] Rheims 2002, p. 19.

a simple person who wants to find, the same as André Breton, "the gold of time" (*l'or du temps*).[36]

"Collectors and museum curators act like treasurers", it is stated and this often is true—too simplistic an opinion for such a complex activity, though. Collecting, both private and public, transcend the individual lives of the human participants: Private collectors withdraw artworks from the circulation at the latest until their death, public collections do that usually forever.[37]

Furthermore, the fact that during the last decades several private collections turn into [public] museums, in many parts of the world, according to the options that each law may provide, is somehow evidence that the line between private and public property was and is constantly being displaced.[38]

The same had happened in the past, especially in USA, but also in Europe, at the last quarter of the 19th century and until the World War II, a period when "extreme collectors" were buying both for themselves and for a museum. Their aim was to accumulate as much art as would be needed for museums of their own, structured at their individual will.

These "collections museums" became public after the collectors' death. Regardless of their differences, they share common elements. As it is perfectly described:

"Is there one name that fits them all? Certainly they should not be called house museums because, though they may appear, superficially, like private houses, they were all intended, from the start, to become public museums of art. Private museums? They are all public. Personal museums? More accurate, because they are personal, even though they are public. Personal art collection museums? Very accurate, but cumbersome. Perhaps collection museum is the best solution, with an occasional reminder that the collection is of art".[39]

1.6 Collecting Contemporary Art

Art objects, as a sub-category of cultural objects, may be considered as having a double identity: private, when they belong to a private collector and public, because of their cultural essence which demands that all people—should have access to them.[40] Being so specific, normally they are regulated by both public and private law—in different quotas, according to the "mentality" of each legal system.

In any case, private collectors who acquire art objects, not only become the owners of them for their own enjoyment but they also possess objects that,

36 Cabanne 2003, p. 8.

37 van der Grijp 2006, p. 8.

38 Higonnet 2010, p. 169.

39 Higonnet 2010, p. xii.

40 Galván Romarate-Zabala 1997, p. 101.

according to a certain opinion, could be considered as part of the artistic treasures of their countries.

Furthermore, collectors have rights and duties, such as: care and conservation of the art objects, loan for exhibitions, taxes for possession or alienation of the art objects, etc.

In most countries—if not all—there is no specific legislation on [private] collecting art, even less on collecting contemporary art. But even in those countries, one may try to locate the rules which concern collectors in the regulations of protection and conservation of cultural objects, alienation of them, import and export, etc.

Is "collecting the new" possible or not? Doubts have been expressed mostly in the past and mostly about collecting the new by museums,[41] since an art object is a creation of an artist but at the same time "a complete narrative unto itself".[42]

Ernst Gombrich was remarking in 1999: "I think that a museum of modern art is a contradiction in terms". The traditional view about museums' objects was that they should have withstood the test of time, so that they could have a particular place in "the future's past". Therefore, contemporary artworks, by entering a museum's collection "are in a sense projected into the future".[43]

Famous examples of museums that were created in the past with the aim to collect and exhibit contemporary paintings are: the room of contemporary paintings, at the opening of the Museo Nacional del Prado, in Madrid, the Musée des Artistes Vivants, in Paris in 1818, the Gallery of Living Art, in USA, at New York University in 1927.

References

Altshuler B (2005) Collecting the new: a historical introduction. In: Altshuler B (ed) Collecting the new. Princeton University Press, Princeton, pp 1–14

Attali J (1997) Mémoire de sabliers. Collections, mode d'emploi. Les Editions de l'Amateur, Paris

Baudrillard J (1994) The system of collecting. In: Elsner J, Cardinal R (eds) The cultures of collecting. Harvard University Press, Cambridge, pp 7–24

Bonneau SG (2013) Honor and destruction: the conflicted object in moral rights law. St. John's Law Rev 87:47–105

Cabanne P (2003) Les grands collectionneurs. Tome I: Du Moyen Age au XIXe siècle. les Editions de l'Amateur, Paris

Carrier D (2006) Museum skepticism. A history of the display of art in public galleries. Duke University Press, Durham

Clowney D (2011) Definitions of art and fine art's historical origins. J Aesthet Art Crit 69:309–320

[41] Altshuler 2005, p. 1, states that Gertrude Stein believed that a museum of contemporary art was impossible.

[42] Bonneau 2013, p. 74.

[43] Altshuler 2005, p. 2.

Galván Romarate-Zabala A (1997) Comercio del arte, arte del comercio: Coleccionismo privado de arte contemporáneo en Madrid (1970–1990), Universidad Complutense de Madrid 1997. http://www.biblioteca.ucm.es/tesis/19972000/H/0/H0042001.pdf

Gómez Pellón E (2011) A propósito del patrimonio cultural del norte de Marruecos: Paradigmas y reflexiones. In: Gómez Pellón E, González Vázquez A (eds) Religión y Patrimonio Cultural en Marruecos. Una aproximación antropológica e histórica. Signatura Demos, pp 67–110

Higonnet A (2010) A museums of one's own. Private collection, public gift. Periscope Publishing, Pittsburgh

Iamandi C (1997) The Charters of Athens 1931 and 1933: coincidence, controversy and convergence. Conserv Manag Archaeol Sites 2:17–28

Laureano A (2014) A brief survey on some essentials of Portuguese museum law. Revista Museologia e Patrimônio 7:3–20

Le Clézio JMG (2011) Les musées sont des mondes. Le Clézio J M G (dir) Les musées sont des mondes. Gallimard/Musée du Louvre éditions, Paris, pp 18–39

McIver Lopes D (2014) Beyond art. Oxford University Press, New York

Mezey N (2007) The Paradoxes of cultural property. Columbia Law Rev 107:2004–2046

Moustaira EN (2006) Relation of law and art [in Greek]. Ant N Sakkoulas Publishers, Athens, Komotini

Moustaira EN (2012) Comparative law and cultural objects [in Greek]. Nomiki Vivliothiki, Athens

Moustakas J (1989) Group Rights in cultural property: justifying strict inalienability. Cornell Law Rev 74:1179–1227

Nafziger JAR, Paterson RK (2014a) Cultural heritage law. In: Nafziger JAR, Paterson RK (eds) Handbook on the law of cultural heritage and international trade. Edward Elgar, Cheltenham, pp 1–18

Nafziger JAR, Paterson RK (2014b) International trade in cultural material. In: Nafziger JAR, Paterson RK (eds) Handbook on the law of cultural heritage and international trade. Edward Elgar, Cheltenham, pp 19–43

Pinna G (2005) Patrimonio culturale, musei e il Codice dei beni culturali. Cassanelli R, Pinna G (a cura di) Lo Stato aCulturale. Intorno al Codice dei Beni Culturali. Jaca Book, Milano, pp 41–69

Rheims M (2002) Les collectionneurs. De la curiosité, de la beauté, du goût, de la mode et de la spéculation. Editions Ramsay, Paris

Said E (1993) Culture and imperialism. Vintage, London

Sandretto Re Rebaudengo P (2011) Il diritto dell'arte a esistere ne diritto. In: Ajani G, Donati A (eds) I diritti dell'arte contemporanea. Umberto Allemandi & C, Torino, pp 89–96

Sax JL (1990) Heritage preservation as a public duty: The Abbé Grégoire and the origins of an idea. Mich Law Rev 88:1142–1169

Schubert K (2009) The Curator's egg. The evolution of the museum concept from the French Revolution to the present day, 3rd edn. Ridinghouse, London

Scott DA (2013) Modern antiquities: the looted and the faked. Int J Cult Prop 20:49–75

Somé R (2007) Anthropologie et art contemporain, une esthétique sociale postmoderne. In: Somé R, Schutz C (dir) Anthropologie, art contemporain et musée: Quels liens? L'Harmattan, Paris, pp 11–26

Svanberg F (2008) Museum narration and the collection machine: or how collections make collector. In: Aronsson P, Nyblom A (eds) NaMu IV, comparing: National Museums, territories, nation-building and change. Linköping University, Norrköping, pp 175–182. http://www.ep.liu.se/ecp/030/

Tsosie R (2009) Who controls native cultural heritage: "Art", "Artifacts", and the right to cultural survival. In: Nafziger JAR, Nicgorski AM (eds) Cultural heritage issues: the legacy of conquest, colonization, and commerce. Martinus Nijhoff Publishers, Leiden, pp 3–36

van der Grijp P (2006) Passion and profit towards an anthropology of collecting. Lit Verlag, Berlin

Chapter 2
Comparative Studies of Civilization—Comparative Studies of Art Collection

2.1 Collectors in Different Parts of the World, in Different Moments of Time

2.1.1 Enrico Cernuschi's Collection—Italy, 19th Century

Enrico Cernuschi was born in Milan but in 1852 was exiled to France because of his republican convictions. He became a wealthy banker in Paris and in 1871 he went for a year to the Far East: Japan, China, Mongolia, Indonesia and India.

He began collecting while in Japan[1] and he continued doing so in the other countries too, except India. When he went back to Paris, he exhibited his treasures in the Palais de l'Industrie, on the occasion of the first Congrès International des Orientalistes, and afterwards he bought land in the French capital in order to build his own museum.

At that time too, Chernuschi purchased the entire collection of Michele Cavaleri, a lawyer from Milan and an old friend of his. The ones who persuaded him to do so, where Giuseppe Ferrari and Carlo Cataneo, under whose tutorship Cernuschi had studied in Italy philosophy of history.

Cattaneo and Ferrari admired Giambattista Vico,[2] the great Italian philosopher of law, the most important work of whom was "I principi di una scienza nuova d'intorno alla commune natura delle nazioni", first published in 1725.

Notwithstanding their admiration for Vico, Cattaneo and Ferrari criticized his work on two counts: firstly, they believed that his cyclical theory of history was narrow and did not take into account the concept of progress; and secondly, they did not like the fact that Vico focused only in the Graeco-Roman and Judaeo-Christian traditions in his studies of the origins of the civilized world.

---

[1] As Davoli 2013, p. 43 states: "It was a favourable time to purchase works of art in Japan. The Meiji Restoration had caused a major religious shift by legally abolishing the syncretism between Buddhism and Shinto and declaring the latter the national religion. Many temples were converted or demolished, and a number of Buddhist statues taken down, abandoned or destroyed".

[2] On Giambattista Vico, as one of the pioneers of comparative law, see Moustaira 2003, pp. 7–9.

E. Moustaira, *Art Collections, Private and Public: A Comparative Legal Study*, SpringerBriefs in Law, DOI 10.1007/978-3-319-15802-0_2

They decided to "complete" Vico's comparative studies of civilizations by analyzing the civilizations of Far East. They used comparative linguistics in their methodology.[3]

Giuseppe Ferrari had been responsible for proposing and supporting the sale of the Cavaleri (himself one of Cattaneo's pupils and admirer of Vico's theories of the philosophy of history) collection to Enrico Cernuschi. Cavaleri's collection consisted primarily of Western art, while Cernuschi's collection comprised only Asian art. Therefore, in Ferrari's view, Cernuschi's purchase of the Cavaleri collection would facilitate the comparative study of art in East and West.[4]

At about 1880, Cernuschi gave up the idea of a comparative study of art in East and West. Nevertheless, the originated in Vico fundamental idea about the influence of the civilizations on the creation of specific art works had already taken roots.

2.1.2 Ernesto Francisco Fenollosa—Japan—USA, 19th–20th Century

In the 1860s, Japanese observers went to the West and they saw for the first time museums, exhibitions, and other institutions of visual culture that were so numerous in Europe and America. Thus, they needed new words with which to describe them, when they went back to Japan.[5] In order to describe the patent office in Washington, the translator of the representatives of Tokugawa government who had gone to USA to ratify commercial treaties between Japan and USA, used the word "hakubutsukan" that literally meant "hall of diverse objects".

The next Japanese missions that went to USA adopted the same name for all kinds of museums and the name was established after it was published in the encyclopedic book "Seiyo Jiyo" (Conditions in the West), written by Fukuzawa Yukichi.

During the last quarter of the 19th century, the extreme desire of "westernization", expressed by many Japanese, had provoked the reaction of many others who were seeing in that unconditional borrowing of any element of Western influence a threat to the unique and traditional country's elements.

Among the Western scholars that were invited at that time in Japan, to teach at the University of Tokio, was Ernest Francisco Fenollosa, who had been born and had studied in Massachusetts.[6] He was invited to teach logics and philosophy.[7]

---

[3] See Davoli 2013, p. 48, stating that Cattaneo had written several articles about India, China, Japan and the Middle East, inspired by the methodology of comparative linguistics.

[4] Davoli 2013, pp. 47–49.

[5] Lockyer 2008, p. 100.

[6] Moustaira 2012, p. 85.

[7] See Moustaira 2010, p. 1677, stating that in the Japanese language there was no term that could translate the term "philosophy" until 1874, when Amane Nishi proposed the term "tetsugaku", that was established ever since.

When Fenollosa went to Japan, many cultural treasures were sold for almost nothing or, worse, were burned, because of the above mentioned will of westernization. Fenollosa started visiting temples in which antiquities and other art objects were stored. In 1881 he founded a club of artists, with the name Kanga-kai. In 1882 he presented a paper praising amongst others the superiority of the Japanese pictorial art versus the imitation of Western models.[8]

In 1886, Fenollosa stopped teaching at the university and was appointed as Commissioner of Fine Arts in Japan. Together with two Japanese colleagues, he went the same year abroad, to study the European methods that were followed in art. Back to Japan, in 1887, they urged for the renaissance of the real Japanese art. It was then that the Art Faculty was inaugurated in Tokyo.

Having already contributed in a significant way to the realization of projects concerning the protection of the Japanese cultural objects, he felt confident that there were others who could be appointed as directors of those works and in 1890 he accepted the proposal by the Fine Arts Museum, Boston, to become curator of the newly founded Department of Asian Art.[9]

2.1.3 Argentina—Municipal Museums, 20th Century

In Argentina, at about the middle of the 20th century,[10] municipal museums were established in small province towns, by initiative of collectors who had in their possession many and various cultural objects, either historical or archaeological or of natural sciences.[11]

These collections had been created in the private sphere and afterwards were ceded to the municipalities, becoming municipal/public museums. All these museums, private and public, were governed by the same (not always written) rules. All of them had their origin in and owed their development to a sole person. This phenomenon was called: "the museum of a sole father" (*el museo de padre único*).

This concept describes exactly the small museums that are generally far away from the big cities and that often have their origin in one sole person.[12] According to a seemingly well-based opinion, even though these museums are characterized by their surprising individuality and the idiosyncratic vision of their creator/collector,

---

[8] Cabeza Lainez and Almodóvar Melendo 2004, p. 75.

[9] Moustaira 2012, p. 87.

[10] In many South American countries, as for example in Argentina, Chile, Peru, museums have been established rather "late" in time (in comparison with the museums of the European countries), that is, at about the end of the 19th century or during the 20th century, following the creation of private collections. Thus, it is stated that in the case of Argentina of the 19th century, according to the mentality of that time fine arts were a superior level which should be pursued only after the material life's necessities would have been satisfied, see Baldasarre 2006, p. 294.

[11] Pupio 2005, pp. 206–207.

[12] Rosso 1991, p. 242.

there are common tendencies in them that require for these museums the recognition of a specific category. These municipal museums had common characteristics not only because they had their origin in the person of a collector, but also because they shared a common patron during the process of selection, interpretation and exhibition of the objects, a process intensified by the strings of relation developed among them.[13]

As it is very well pointed out, the nature of these institutions does not correspond to any of the museums categories that other scholars make. For example, Krysztof Pomian, speaking about the formation of public museums, distinguishes four models[14]: the "traditional", represented by institutions which were developed as the continuation of collections and that were open to the public at certain occasions; the "revolutionary", that is, museums established by decrees and controlled by the State; the "benefactor", the collections of which had been donated by the proprietaries after their death; and the "commercial", formed by purchase of collections. In the case of these Argentinian museums, the State had accepted the donation of the collections but at the same time permitted that their control remained under the supervision of the donators.[15]

The collectors that were at the origin of these municipal museums were seeing themselves as "dilettanti" and not at all professionals. Many of them had collected archaeological material during field trips, something contrary to the law (Law 9080 of 1913/1921) that at that time was governing archaeological objects and that was declaring property of the nation the archaeological and paleontological ruins and sites of scientific interest and was conferring to the Ministry of Justice and Public Instruction (*Ministerio de Justicia e Instrucción Pública*) the competence to grant permits—only to local or foreign scientific institutions—for the use and exploitation of those sites, with the advice of the following museums: Museo Nacional de Historia Natural, Museo Etnográfico de la Facultad de Filosofía y Letras de la Universidad de Buenos Aires and Museo de la Plata.

The constitutional reform for the provinces of Argentina, of 1949, had created a new administrative design. The Ministry of Education was created that year and its action was divided in 3 sub-secretariats, competent for the: (a) Administration, (b) Education, (c) Culture. In the frame of the third, the Dirección de Museos Históricos was created, converted in 1953 to the Dirección de Museos, Reservas e Investigaciones Culturales.

In this institutional context, as it is pointed out, the collectors chose different strategies in order to make their collections public, trying at the same time to show that they were leading this decision.[16]

---

[13] Farró Fonalleras 1995, p. 54.

[14] Pomian 1987.

[15] Pupio 2005, p. 207 n. 3.

[16] Pupio 2005, pp. 212–214.

2.2 Models of Cultural Politics

What is cultural politics? A definition of general acceptance is that it is "a moment of convergence y coherence between, on the one side, the role that the State may represent in the art and the "culture" in relation with the society, and on the other side, the organization of a public action".

According to another definition, proposed by a Mexican scholar, cultural politics is the total of initiatives of the State, the private institutions and the associations of communities that have as their aims to orient the symbolic development, to answer to the cultural exigencies of the countries and to achieve consensus on a form of order or social change.[17]

The term cultural politics was "invented" by the French Ministry of Cultural Affairs, in 1959, and more specifically by the Minister and great literary man, André Malreaux. Since the beginning, the inspiration was a governmental intervention with a will for social reform.

In the European space, during the second half of the 20th century, this intervention took the form of various and not identical between them definitions. Kulturpolitik, in Germany, covering artistic, educative and entertaining activities, politica culturale dei beni culturali, in Italy, specifically referring to the protection of cultural objects, *arts policy*, in England, mainly associated with the mass entertainment and the cultural industries.

This variety of definitions and descriptions is the proof that the term cultural politics and its meaning is heavily conditioned by the historic and politic context into which it is developed, having as result a big variety of aims and institutional forms,[18] the comparison of which is very difficult.

Most of the scholars speak about two big models which have become references on a universal level. These two models are, on the one hand the model of the intervening State that has the most important duties and responsibilities on the development of the cultural sector, and on the other hand the model of the USA which is composed by big cultural and patrimonial institutions, autonomous and private.[19]

In the Latin American space, cultural politics has been the field of studies mainly anthropological and of communication and cultural mediation. During the 90s, the center of attention for those who do research on cultural studies and more specifically cultural politics in Latin America, is a "critical conceptualization", that is, an interdisciplinary ambit, originated in England but with various influences by Marxism, Frankfurt's School and critical theory. In Latin America, this amalgam of

[17] "El conjunto de intervenciones realizadas por el Estado, las instituciones civiles y los groupos comunitarios organizados a fin de orientar el desarrollo simbólico, satisfacer las necesitades culturales de la población y obtener consenso para un tipo de orden o transformación social", see García Canclini 1987, p. 13.

[18] Zamorano and Rius Ulldemolins and Klein 2014, p. 6.

[19] Muñoz 2014, p. 55.

theories was also influenced by the sociological and anthropological studies on indigenism.

In Brazil, there have been observed, in the passage of time, various grades of participation of the State and of the political, economic and social elites in the sector of culture. It is openly recognized that other factors too influence the choices that a state makes, as far as its participation is concerned.

Such factors are the organization of the civil society, the formation of a conscience from the part of the business community and the civil society about the social importance of the investment in certain cultural areas, especially those that are connected to a national, regional or local tradition and the relation of culture with the education.[20]

In Brazil, as in other countries too, the constitution of a distinct area of "culture" was closely connected to the will of preserving a national cultural property and of fortifying a national identity. During the 20th century, there were various programs concerning the protection of culture.

In 1991, a law (Lei Rouanet[21]) established the "Programa Nacional de Apoio à Cultura". On the one hand, it signified the effort of some intellectuals to promote culture which had been financially debilitated and on the other hand, enactment of this law was a sort of affirmation of the dominant tendency in the frame of the Federal Government to redirect the financing of culture to the economic market.

According to other comparative studies about cultural politics in various Western countries, that have been published about 20 years ago, there are three models of that cultural politics: the European continental model, the Nordic model and the Anglosaxon liberal model.

In the first, European continental model, there exists a structure of excellency-oriented artistic institutions and at the same time there is a strong tradition of public intervention. A clear example of this model is France.

In these countries, the predominant model is that according to which the culture sector is governed either directly by the State or indirectly by organisms depending on the public administration. As a rule, in these countries artistic institutions are subsidized and their management is controlled by public representatives who, among other responsibilities, have to choose the directors of those institutions.

In the Nordic countries, where the social democrat model of the welfare state has been fully developed, the cultural action of the State has a predominant role, nevertheless it is not really normative, nor does it follow a hierarchy, it is rather universalistic and equalitarian. The polyvalent cultural centers that exist in these countries are a clear expression of this model.

In the case of countries following the liberal model, it is the private sector which traditionally supports cultural institutions. The market regulates cultural life, the management organs are independent, and the State's intervention is minor.

---

20 Abreu 2010, p. 167.

21 From the name of the then Secretary of Culture, Sérgio Paulo Rouanet, see Abreu 2010, p. 179.

There are countries, in which different models are followed. Such is the case of Spain, according to a scholar: Madrid follows the European continental model, while Barcelona shows a tendency to follow the liberal model, with institutions that had started by private initiative.

According to another opinion, one observes a tendency of convergence between the different models. The appearance of contracts-programs in countries following various models of cultural politics could constitute evidence of this tendency to convergence between models, in accordance with the theory of institutional isomorphism of mimetic character.[22]

2.3 Art Education Policy—Comparative Cultural Policy

Art education policy as a sub-field of comparative cultural policy is an important research field for those who are interested in the regulation of private collections and public museums. During the last 20 years it has been foreseen and in the end confirmed, that all "policy issues related to the arts and culture" have taken on "an added, cross-national dimension".[23]

What is a comparative cultural policy? The approaches are divided, just like the approaches to the definition of culture, which may follow either an anthropological or an aesthetic pattern. Thus, some scholars follow an anthropological, critical approach to cultural policy research, focusing on cultural theory and cultural studies, while others follow an applied approach to this research, based on public policy and political science research methods.[24]

The concept of cultural policy, adopted by the 2005 UNESCO Convention on the Protection and Promotion of the Diversity of Cultural Expression*s*, is the following:

"Cultural policies and measures" refers to those policies and measures relating to culture, whether at the local, national, regional or international level that are either focused on culture as such or are designed to have a direct effect on cultural expressions of individuals, groups or societies, including on the creation, production, dissemination, distribution of and access to cultural activities, goods, and services.

Various studies appear, handling among other issues the possible impact of cultural diversity on the cultural policy of the States. "Does cultural diversity imply the end of national cultures?", they are asking[25] and they try to elaborate on the different attitudes of various countries towards this phenomenon.

---

[22] Rubio Arostegui and Rius Ulldemolins 2012, pp. 14–15.

[23] Kawashima 1995, p. 289.

[24] Dewey 2008, p. 279.

[25] Bonet and Négrier 2011, p. 574.

Declaring that cultural diversity has become an important consideration for artistic directors too, they argue about the approach to questions of cultural diversity by [mostly] Western European countries, concluding that the differences in practice among these countries are neither stable nor absolute and acknowledging the "uncertainty that surrounds its definition", the "ambivalence and the dilemmas which it creates".[26]

References

Abreu R (2010) A cultura do mecenato no Brasil: uma utopia possível? In: Nascimento Junior J Do (org.) Economia de museus, Brasilia, Ministerio da Cultura; Instituto Brasileiro de Museus. pp 163–201

Baldasarre MI (2006) Sobre los inicios del coleccionismo y los museos de arte en la Argentina. Anais do Museu Paulista 14:293–321

Bonet L, Négrier E (2011) The end(s) of national cultures? Cultural policy in the face of diversity. Int J Cult Policy 17:574–589

Cabeza Lainez JM, Almodóvar Melendo JM (2004) Ernest Francisco Fenollosa and the Quest for Japan. Findings of a life devoted to the science of art. Bull Portuguese/Jpn Stud 9:75–99

Davoli S (2013) Comparing east and west: Enrico Cernuschi's collections of art reconsidered. In: Bracken S, Gáldy AM, Turpin A (eds) Collecting east and west. Cambridge Scholars Publishing, Newcastle Upon Tyne, pp 41–59

Dewey P (2008) A comparative approach to art education policy research. Stud Art Educ 49:277–293

Farró Fonalleras D (1995) Collectors and their museums: towards a specific typology. Museum Int 47:54–58

García Canclini N (1987) Introducción. Políticas Culturales y crisis de desarrollo: un balance latinoamericano. In: García Canclini N, Bonfil G (eds) Políticas Culturales en América Latina. Grijalbo, México, pp 13–61

Kawashima N (1995) Comparing cultural policy: towards the development of comparative study cultural. Policy 1:289–307

Lockyer A (2008) National museums and other cultures in modern Japan. In: Sherman DJ (ed) Museums and difference. Indiana University Press, Bloomington, pp 97–123

Moustaira EN (2003) The milestones of comparative law. Thesis and Antithesis [in Greek]. Ant.N. Sakkoulas Publ., Athens

Moustaira EN (2010) Comparative law—Comparative aesthetics [in Greek]. In: Volume in honor of Prof.M.P. Stathopoulos. Ant.N. Sakkoulas Publ., Athina, pp 1673–1683

Moustaira EN (2012) Comparative law and cultural objects [in Greek]. Nomiki Vivliothiki, Athens

Muñoz N (2014) Propuesta para abordar la cultura desde un análisis comparativo de política pública. Políticas Públicas 53–66

Pomian K (1987) Collectionneurs, amateurs et curieux. Gallimard, Paris, Paris-Venise, XVIe-XVIIIe siècle

Pupio MA (2005) Coleccionistas de objetos históricos, arqueológicos y de ciencias naturales en museos municipales de la provincia de Buenos Aires en la década de 1950. História, Ciências, Saúde 12(suplemento):205–229

Rosso AD (1991) In central Argentina: a single-parent museum. Museum Int 43:242–244

[26] Bonet and Négrier 2011, pp. 575–587.

Rubio Arostegui JA, Rius Ulldemolins J (2012) La modernización de la gestión pública de la cultura. Análisis comparado del caso de los equipamientos culturales de las comunidades autónomas de Cataluña y Madrid. Revista Gestión y Análisis de Políticas Públicas 8:11–34

Zamorano MM, Rius Ulldemolins J, Klein R (2014) ¿Hacia un modelo sudamericano de política cultural? Singularidades y convergencias en Uruguay, Paraguay y Chile en el siglo XXI. Revista Europea de Estudios Latinoamericanos y del Caribe 96:5–34

Chapter 3
Collectors' Rights "Versus" Artists' Rights—Conservation and Collection Care

3.1 General Comments

In civil-law countries such as France, owners of artworks that are considered significant parts of the cultural heritage of the country, may have an implied legal duty to maintain the integrity of the work, whereas in common-law countries like the USA and the United Kingdom, personal property rights often are a hurdle to any obligation to protect an artwork (moral rights aside). In theory, a US owner of a rare Picasso could set it on fire, if desired.

In USA, most serious collectors of significant works of art like to consider themselves as custodians of the art works they possess, taking care of these treasures for future generations. It is argued that, investment value aside, the obligation to care for important works of art is rather an ethical one.[1] This is not always the case, though.[2]

Until fairly recently, in USA, collectors' rights were not at all "threatened" by artists' rights. The so called droit moral, that is, the artists' continuing interest in their work, was not easy to be accepted by U.S. legal mentality, legal culture.[3]

At some point, in the late 1970s and 80s, this mentality changed. USA had acquired new wealth and power after the World War II and Abstract Expressionists had "transferred" the center of the Western art world from Paris to New York. These facts had contributed to the rise of the cultural importance of American art. Almost a natural consequence of this was that the U.S. decided to enact statutes

---

[1] Rozell 2014, p. 145.

[2] See Costonis 2000, p. 1847, reviewing the book of *Joseph Sax*, "Playing Darts ..." (see next footnote): "Many [collectors] see themselves as stewards, self-obligated to protect the art and even to loan it out for public viewing from time to time. Were all collectors similarly inclined, Sax would eschew a formal legal regime mandating periodic display of their master works. Not all collectors, however, are so inclined".

[3] Sax 1999, p. 21.

E. Moustaira, *Art Collections, Private and Public: A Comparative Legal Study*, SpringerBriefs in Law, DOI 10.1007/978-3-319-15802-0_3

consecrating the "moral rights", both at the federal and state level, mostly following the European civil law model(s).[4]

Furthermore, there were some States that also granted to the artist a right against destruction, mutilation, alteration of his/her work. California, first (California Civil Code, Section 989) and Massachusetts, following California (Massachusetts Statutes, Chapter 231, Section 85S), have gone even further and in their laws expressly command private owners (collectors) to preserve works of art for the benefit of public.

Copyright law—and especially the part concerning visual artists—is, by all means, a hot issue in common law countries. Some scholars, opposite to its strictness, contend that its originality requirements rely on a romantic conception of a genius creator.[5] Nevertheless, there are scholars in the opposite, romantic-bias camp.[6]

As it is pointed out, a bit harshly, "The copyright laws of both the United States and the United Kingdom explicitly agree on at least one doctrine: When law and art chance a meeting, they should do their best to avoid each other".[7] Both countries' courts try to remain aesthetically neutral. There are several reasons for that and the fact that judges lack special knowledge about art is not the least of them.[8]

3.2 Moral Rights

Scholars in USA often refer to a divide between author-oriented civil law countries and user-oriented common law countries. This divide has been historically marked by the presence or absence of moral rights in copyright law.[9]

In 1990, the U.S. Copyright Act was amended and [only] visual artists were named possessors of "moral rights". According to the Visual Artists Rights Act of 1990, visual artists enjoy the same protection as authors. Numerous articles were written on this law.[10] Several scholars considered this novelty as at least strange, since copyright was always concerning texts.[11]

The term "moral right" was adopted as the direct translation of the French term "droit moral", which was established in the nineteenth century. Still, there are

---

[4] Merryman 1976, p. 1042, was asking: "Given the cultural importance of American art, should our law be modified in such a way as to protect the integrity of works of art? I believe that the answer to that question is clearly 'yes'".

[5] Barron 2002, p. 368.

[6] Ginsburg 2003, p. 1063.

[7] Fenzel 2007, p. 546.

[8] Farley 2005, pp. 815–819.

[9] Bonneau 2013, p. 48.

[10] Liemer 2005, p. 1.

[11] Tushnet 2012, p. 685.

voices pointing out that the so called moral rights[12] could follow the German term "Urheberpersönlichkeitsrecht" and be called or rather described as authorial rights of personality.[13]

According to an even more specific statement, the French singular term droit moral, which stems from the notion that some of the artist's spirit is injected into his or her creations, "connotes an indivisible package of rights, as distinguished from the plural 'moral rights', reflective of the current American concept of divisibility".[14]

In numerous countries moral rights have been guaranteed since many years, following mainly the French conceptual paradigm, not being identical the legal regulations of all the civil law countries though.[15]

While in Europe it was philosophical ideas about personhood that dominated the moral rights theory, in USA the theory was "rationalized with societal goals",[16] since certain scholars believed that the concept of *droit moral* was inconsistent with the economic-based rights theories that were and always are governing in USA.[17]

Are the differences between the [at least] two mentalities really big? Some scholars deny that, they argue that the distinction between civil and common law countries is more conceptual than practical.[18]

It seems, though, that the differences of legal *mentality* are not small. In USA it is the utilitarian rationale that governs intellectual property rights too.[19] Consequently, the focus of the Congress was not on rewarding ownership of right, but primarily on giving economic incentives[20] and thus encouraging future creation.[21]

Some U.S. scholars even state that in our era "of factory-made, industrially fabricated, assistant-produced artwork",[22] moral rights are increasingly acquiring the economic aspects of trademark law.[23]

According to the French legal theory, an artist's rights have economic and personal aspects. The latter, which are embodied in the *droit moral*, predominate over the former.

---

12 The artists' creative minds and souls as embodied in their works, see Applebaum 1992, p. 183.

13 Munzer and Raustiala 2009, p. 68.

14 *Nimmer on Copyright* § 8D.01[A] n.4 (2010), cited by Prowda 2013, p. 101 n. 3.

15 Dworkin 1995, p. 230.

16 Bonneau 2013, p. 52.

17 Cotter 1997, p. 1.

18 Rigamonti 2007, pp. 72–73.

19 Rector 2010, pp. 584–585.

20 Ng 2009, p. 422.

21 Moore 2003, p. 612.

22 Tang 2012, p. 229.

23 Certain scholars have similarly expressed about the connection of literary works and trademark law: they have argued that the attribution right for literary works derives from trade mark law, see: Ginsburg 2005, p. 381; Heymann 2005, p. 1377.

Under French law there are four moral rights,[24] the following:

(a) The Right of Disclosure (*Droit de divulgation*), Code de la propriété intellectuelle, Article L. 212-2.
The artist has the right to decide when a work is finished and when it can be shown. The law applies to original works and to reproductions.
(b) The Right to Withdraw from Publication or to Make Modifications (*Droit de retrait ou de repentir*), Code de la propriété intellectuelle, Article L. 121-4.
It is rather the author of a written work who has this right. He or she can repent or retake a work at any time in exchange for payment.
(c) The Right of Attribution (*Droit à la paternité*), Code de la propriété intellectuelle, Article L. 121-1.
This right has evolved into three distinct rights: First, the right of creators to be recognized as the authors of their works or to publish anonymously or pseudonymously; second, the right to prevent their works to be attributed to someone else; third, the right to prevent the use of their names on works that are not theirs.
(d) The Right of Integrity (*Droit ou respect de l'oeuvre*), Code de la propriété intellectuelle, Article L. 121-1.
The artists have the right to protect their works from distortion, mutilation, transformation, or alteration without their consent, even if they do no longer own the works. This last right is considered as the most essential moral right.

According to most U.S. scholars, moral rights are divided into three categories: the right of integrity, the right of attribution, and the right of disclosure.[25] Other scholars divide them further, either into five categories (attribution, integrity, disclosure, withdrawal, and resale royalties)[26] or into four categories (rights of publication, paternity, integrity, and withdrawal).[27]

UK amended its law in 1988, to comply with the Berne Convention. Until then, it had no moral rights legislation.[28]

Thus, since 1988, Copyright, Designs and Patents Act (CDPA), Chapter IV, Sections 77–89, recognizes four moral rights, the first two of which were introduced to satisfy the UK's obligations under Article 6bis of the Berne Convention. These four moral rights, as it is stated,[29] are the following:

---

[24] Prowda 2013, pp. 102–105.

[25] Rosenthal Kwall 2001, p. 152.

[26] Liemer 1998, pp. 45–46.

[27] Dine 1995, p. 550.

[28] See Prowda 2013, p. 114. She points out that before 1988, plaintiffs sometimes requested courts to fashion a sort of moral right through the laws of defamation, passing off, contract, and Section 43 of the Copyright Act of 1956 (false attributions of authorship).

[29] Prowda 2013, pp. 114–115.

(a) Sections 77–79 (paternity right): The right to be identified as author of a copyrighted … artistic work, as the director of a copyrighted … artistic work…
(b) Sections 80–83 (integrity right): The right of an author or director not to have a work subjected to derogatory treatment if the treatment amounts to distortion or mutilation of the work or is otherwise prejudicial to the honour or reputation of the author or director.
(c) Section 84: The right of a person, in certain circumstances, not to have a[n] … artistic work (whether or not a copyrighted work) falsely attributed to him or her as the author or director.
(d) Section 85: The right of a person who, for private or domestic purposes, commissions the taking of a copyrighted photograph or the making of a copyrighted film, in certain circumstances, not to have copies of those works issued to the public or exhibited or show in public.

Under the law (CDPA Chapter 48, § 78), in the event of infringement, the author of an artistic work must have asserted the right of paternity in agreements with art dealers and ensure that third parties are also bound. In case of a public exhibition of artwork, the author has to be identified on the original, authorized copy or frame.[30]

3.2.1 The Moral Right of Integrity

Usually one can easily see the differences between the national laws, even between the laws of countries which could be considered as more related to each other, according to the classic though outdated taxonomy in families of law. For example, as far as the moral right of integrity is concerned, which requires the purchaser to respect the work in its original form, one observes different attitudes in the various national laws.

In France moral rights are perpetual but still they belong to the person of the artist. The artist's heirs are presumed to inherit only a right of enforcement.[31] In Germany no perpetual right of integrity is recognized, because they believe that by recognizing the right as perpetual, they would convert it into an instrument of cultural preservation.[32]

In USA, the first time that the moral right of integrity was invocated by a court, was in 1949, when a New York court, judging about the destruction of an art object, rejected the artist's moral rights argument, but referenced two writings in its

---

[30] Prowda 2013, p. 115, states that there is not much case law on moral rights in UK and that the moral rights cases have rarely succeeded.

[31] Dietz 1995, p. 214.

[32] Rigamonti 2006, pp. 370–371.

opinion, a law journal article and a treatise: both of them were addressing destruction of art works.

The first writing was arguing that while deforming an artist's work would have as result presenting him [the artist] as the creator of a work that was not his own, destroying his work would not have that result.[33]

The second writing was asserting the opposite, since "the maintenance and preservation of a work of art is invested with the public interest in culture and the development of the arts".[34]

Public interest's importance was reflected already in the artists' rights or art preservation statutes enacted by the states—eleven at the time VARA was enacted: Massachusetts, Connecticut, California, New York, Maine, Louisiana, New Jersey, Illinois, Pennsylvania, New Mexico, Rhode Island. Scholars are confirming that VARA serves "the public interest in preserving its culture through preserving art".[35]

Section 106A(a)(3) provides authors of works of visual art the rights:

> (A) to prevent any intentional distortion … or …modification of that work which would be prejudicial to his or her honor or reputation, and any intentional distortion … or modification of that work is a violation of that right, and (B) to prevent any destruction of a work of recognized stature, and any intentional or grossly negligent destruction of that work is a violation of that right.[36]

Some scholars believe that, by providing such a right, VARA exceeds the norms of all civil and common law countries as well as the Berne's Convention's requirements.[37] Others argue that it is not a functional preservation statute.[38]

The aim of this controversial inclusion of the "recognized stature"—a provision that does not exist in any other national law—for protection against destruction of an artwork was, as it is stated, "to keep out frivolous suits by only acknowledging work of recognized quality as determined by the artistic community".[39]

Anyhow, it seems that there is almost a consensus between the scholars commenting on VARA provisions, that by establishing art preservation as an important purpose, the statute adopts a museological stance.

Interesting seems the difference between U.S. Copyright Act as amended by VARA and U.K. moral rights regulation.[40]

---

[33] Roeder 1940, p. 569.

[34] Ladas 1938.

[35] Bock 2011, p. 162.

[36] VARA only states what destruction or modification is *not*, holding conservation and relocation efforts acceptable "modifications" of an artwork that do not actually *destroy* it, 17 U.S.C. Section 106A(c)(1)–(2), see Tischler 2012, p. 1698 n. 265.

[37] Bonneau 2013, p. 69.

[38] Tipton 2009, p. 274.

[39] Butera 2010, p. 127.

[40] Fenzel 2007, pp. 569–570.

While U.S. Copyright Act limits moral rights to a narrow class of visual artists (creators of works of "recognized stature"), the 1988 Copyright, Designs and Patents Act currently in force in the United Kingdom[41] extends moral rights to all copyright works protected—artistic works included.

However, as it is pointed out, the U.K. copyright regime contains broad exceptions and qualifications, as well as provisions that make moral rights easier waived than according to U.S. law.[42]

In Australian law, the moral rights provisions are a relatively recent addition: they constitute Part IX of the Copyright Act and they came into force on 21 December 2000. These moral rights subsist in—among other works—artistic works (s. 189).

The author is granted three moral rights:

a. The right of attribution of authorship.
b. The right not to have authorship falsely attributed.
c. The right of integrity of authorship.

As far as this third right is concerned, that is, the right not to have works subjected to "derogatory treatment", according to the Australian law (ss 195 AJ to 195 AL), the term "derogatory treatment" covers the following situations:

a. doing something that results in a 'material distortion of', 'mutilation of' or 'material alteration to' a work that is 'prejudicial to the author's honour or reputation';
b. doing any other act that is 'prejudicial to the author's honour or reputation';
c. exhibiting an artistic work in public in a way that is 'prejudicial to the author's honour or reputation because of the manner or place in which the exhibition occurs'.

However, it is considered that there is no infringement of rights of integrity in two cases: first, when the act was 'reasonable' (ss 195 AR, 195 AS)[43] and second, if it is an act or omission that falls within the ambit of a written consent provided by the holder of moral rights in a work (ss 195 AW, 195 AWA).

3.2.2 Moral Rights—Aboriginal Art

According to Australian law, moral rights can only be held by natural people (s 190) and they "focus on the personality and emotional needs of the creating artist

[41] It applies to the whole of the United Kingdom—England, Wales, Scotland and Northern Ireland (Copyright, Designs and Patents Act, § 157.

[42] Dworkin 1995, pp. 245–263.

[43] And the Copyright Act sets out factors for determining whether the act was 'reasonable', see Hudson 2006, pp. 68–70.

and on the uniqueness of the created object". This individualistic characteristic of the moral rights creates problems as far as the protection of aboriginal art is concerned, an art based on ideas about communal creation and ownership.[44]

It is argued that even though the current moral rights provisions are based on notions of individual ownership, they could be of benefit for the indigenous communities, enforced in a way consistent with indigenous laws and practices. As an example, it is stated that the integrity right may serve to prevent reproduction or display in a manner that would be culturally insensitive.[45]

It has been repeatedly commented that communal rights should be explicitly recognized in Australian copyright law. In 2003, the government prepared a draft with possible amendments to the Copyright Act, by acceptance of which communal moral rights would be recognized. However, this bill was never introduced into parliament.[46]

New Zealand intellectual property regime,[47] on the other side, "is unique in containing provisions that are intended to partially address the ethical, cultural, and ownership issues of its indigenous culture" (Trade Marks Act 2002, s. 17(c) and Patents Bill 2008, cl 14.).[48]

3.2.3 *Case VARA Precedent? MASS MoCA V. Christoph Büchel*

In 2006, the Massachusetts Museum of Contemporary Art[49] invited Swiss artist Büchel to create a thematic work for its Building 5, one of the largest galleries of any museum in USA.[50] Büchel's proposal was for a large-scale work, an installation, called "Training Ground for Democracy", with detailed scenarios in which counter-terrorist forces might find themselves within USA and in other countries. The aim was to construct "a mini theater of war", evoking the experience of US military forces by mimicking the U.S. Army's virtual trainings.[51]

The collaboration had problems from the start. Mass MoCA was trying to formalize the working relationship through a signed written proposal by the artist, who was avoiding it. The artist was proposing a contract requiring the museum to transport and organize the material for the installation. Subsequently, the project

[44] Loughlan 2002, pp. 19–20.

[45] Hudson 2006, p. 69.

[46] Janke 2005, p. 107.

[47] Corbett 2012a, p. 882.

[48] Corbett 2012b, pp. 920–921.

[49] Which, as stated, has gained a reputation as one of the most adventurous contemporary museums, see Rector 2010, p. 580.

[50] Telesetsky 2008, p. 87.

[51] Rector 2010, p. 581.

was well over budget, since Büchel, in order to complete the installation, requested a movie theater interior, a house, a bar, a mobile home, sea cargo containers, a variety of vehicles, an aircraft fuselage, and a bomb carousel.

By the end of January 2007, the Mass MoCA director decided to continue the project, with or without Büchel, in order to prepare an exhibit that would have the title "Made in Mass MoCA". According to the museum, the collaboration could not continue because the artist was "impossible". According to the artist, the museum was putting obstacles to the expression of his artistic vision, so he asserted that he "will not accept any orders and any more pressure or compromises as to how things have been done from the museum director or museum's technicians".

On May 21, 2007, the museum requested a declaratory judgment[52] from the District Court of Massachusetts to permit it to display the materials and non-completed constructions in Building 5.

In response to the museum's filing of a legal complaint, Büchel filed a counterclaim seeking money damages under VARA and a declaration prohibiting the museum from unveiling the installation. Both sides moved for summary judgment[53]—"a part of modern discovery-driven litigation", which is quite often followed in art disputes cases and which has as a consequence the vanishing of the trial.[54]

Mass MoCA argued that it owned the materials in the installation, that it had collected donations for the exhibition, purchased the remaining components of the installations with its funds and that it was its staff or contractors those who constructed the work. Furthermore, it argued that the artwork was unfinished, therefore no title or copyright should transfer to the artist, and that VARA does not apply, since display of a work that does not exist does not constitute distortion, mutilation, or modification.

Büchel's arguments were that: (a) VARA protects an artist's *moral rights* for works that are still in progress; (b) Büchel's proposed exhibition was one of the types of visual art that VARA intended to protect; (c) unfinished works of visual art have the same protection as finished artworks; (d) if the museum would show the work as it was, it would distort Büchel's reputation as an artist; and (e) the museum willfully distorted and modified his work by continuing to work on it after the artist had made clear that he would no longer agree to that.

The U.S. District Court for the District Court of Massachusetts upheld the museum's request for declaratory relief.[55] It agreed with the museum that it could display the unfinished installation with a disclaimer that the work does not represent

52 "The implications of this case regarding the shifting dynamics between artists and institutions are enormous, especially as institutions move into the role of producing and financing the creation of artworks rather than just exhibit them", Gover 2012, p. 46.

53 Telesetsky 2008, p. 89.

54 Redish 2005, p. 1329.

55 Mass. Museum of Contemporary Art Found., Inc. v. Büchel, 565 F. Supp.2d 245 (D. Mass. 2008).

a finished work of art by Büchel. He also ruled that neither the Copyright Act nor VARA would prohibit a museum from works that it would identify as unfinished.

Büchel's attorneys immediately appealed the decision to the First Circuit. The appellate court disagreed with the district court's analysis. It held that a work in progress could be protected under VARA if it is "fixed" so that it "is sufficiently permanent or stable to permit it to be perceived, reproduced, or otherwise communicated for a period of more than transitory duration".

The First Circuit Court mentioned its approval to the Second Circuit for its implicit finding in the case Carter v. Helmsley-Spear, Inc.,[56] that VARA could apply to an unfinished sculpture being installed in a building lobby.[57]

It held that VARA does apply to the partially completed "Training Ground for Democracy" and went on to evaluate rights of attribution and integrity. On the first, there was no need of reviewing the injunctive relief because the installation had already been dismantled. On the right of integrity, it concluded that there were disputes that should have been resolved by the jury at the district court level of review.[58]

The standards of contemporary art today are different than those of the time when VARA was drafted and enacted. It is rightly pointed out that "installation art became prominent in the 1990s, resulting in larger-scale museum exhibitions".[59] Judgments like the one of the U.S. District Court for the District Court of Massachusetts exclude artworks that the statute had not explicitly addressed because they did not exist at that time.[60]

3.3 Droit de Suite—Resale Royalty—Resale Right

"Over the centuries, great wealth in the arts has rarely been translated into great wealth for the artist". On the contrary, at least in the past the poverty of the artists was in contrast with the wealth of the buyers of their artworks. What was meant to remedy this injustice, the primarily French "droit de suite", the resale royalty right[61]—a right that entitles the artist to a portion of a higher subsequent sale price —is currently recognized in 79 countries (jurisdictions), but only in California in USA.[62]

In France, advocates of artists had asked since 1893 for a resale right to be recognized. At last, and because of the public pressure, a *droit de suite*, a resale

[56] 71 F. 3d 77 (2nd Cir. 1995).

[57] Telesetsky 2011, p. 256.

[58] Telesetsky 2011, p. 257.

[59] Rector 2010, p. 598.

[60] Wu 2009, p. 151.

[61] Price 1968, pp. 1334–1335.

[62] Kumar 2014, p. 444.

royalty right for artists was adopted in 1920. It granted French visual artists a 3 % royalty upon resale of their works.

More countries followed, mainly European but not only—for example, Brazil, Chile, Costa Rica, Ivory Coast.

In Spanish law, the "Derecho de participación" was first regulated by Article 24 of the Real Decreto Legislativo 1/1996. In Italy the "diritto di seguito" was formally introduced by the Articles 144–155 of the Law 633/1941.[63] Unfortunately, it was never applied because of the complexity of the procedure of the sales' regulation and the absence of real powers of control, of inspection of its application.

In 1971, when the 1886 Berne Convention for the Protection of Literary and Artistic Works—the fundamental principle of which was national treatment[64] —was revised at Paris, a new provision was added, encouraging Member States to codify "the inalienable right to an interest in any sale of the work subsequent to the first transfer by the author of the work".[65]

In the frame of European Union, the problems of this right's application in some countries and the normative silence in others had as result a complete lack of homogeneity in the art market. Many commercial transactions of art objects were being concluded in an opportunistic way, in countries where the resale royalty was not regulated.[66]

Having been considered as a matter of great importance, needing harmonization, the Directive 2001/84/CE of the European Parliament and the European Council was promulgated. According to the Article 12 of the Directive, the Member States had to adopt the necessary legal regulations in order to fulfill its content, until 1 January 2006.

As mentioned above, some Member States had already adopted measures introducing this right, even if some of them could not always apply it: Belgium, Denmark, France, Germany, Greece, Sweden, Spain, Italy.

Not every Member State respected the time limit set by the Directive. For example, Spain took such initiative only in 2008 and approved the Law 3/2008 "relativa al Derecho de Participación en beneficio del autor de una obra de arte original".[67]

Italy introduced the Directive with the Law Decree 118/13.2.2006, "Attuazione della direttiva 2001/84/CE, relative al diritto d'autore di un'opera d'arte sulle successive vendite dell'originale".

The right applies only in cases of public sales concluded by professional operators of the art market, but not between private persons or with non-profit

[63] Favretto 2007, p. 164.

[64] Brauneis 2013.

[65] Plaisant 1987, p. 157.

[66] Favretto 2007, p. 164.

[67] *Sobre el estatuto jurídico tributario del coleccionista en España y posibles medidas que contribuyan a su promoción*, Informe de la Fundación Arte y Mecenazgo, Barcelona 2014, p. 34.

institutions. It is recognized for all citizens of the UE countries, while for citizens of third countries it is recognized only on the condition of reciprocity.

The right does not apply when the professional seller has acquired the artwork directly by the artist/author during the 3 years before such sale and when the sale's price is not superior that 10.000 euros.

In USA, where there were—and still are—many opponents to the idea of the artists' poverty,[68] the only state, so far, that has enacted legislation providing artists with a right to recover royalties upon the subsequent resale of their original works, subject to certain conditions, is California.[69]

The California Resale Royalty Act was enacted in 1976. An American artist, that is, anyone who "at the time of resale, is a citizen of the United States, or a resident of the state who has resided in the state for a minimum of 2 years",[70] must be paid a 5 % royalty of the total sales price "when a work of fine art is sold at auction or by a gallery, dealer, broker, museum" and "the seller resides in California or the sale takes place in California".[71] Upon the death of the artist, the right is transferred to the artist's heirs for a period of 20 years.[72]

In May 2012, a California federal court ruled that the California Resale Royalty Act was unconstitutional under the Commerce Clause.[73] More specifically, it concluded that the Act violated the "Dormant Commerce Clause". This is not an explicit clause of the U.S. Constitution, it rather "describes the extent to which states are prohibited, by virtue of the Commerce Clause, from passing laws that regulate or unduly burden interstate commerce" because this is Congress's competence.[74]

This first instance ruling is awaiting a decision on appeal by the Ninth Circuit Court of Appeals.[75]

The opponents to a state or a federal legislation consecrating a resale royalty argue that the primary market for fine art is very competitive—in USA there are more than 6,000 galleries and art dealers[76]—and consequently visual artist are not really in a poor bargaining position.[77]

Still, many are the supporters of the enactment of a federal resale royalty law that would amend the U.S. Copyright Act. So far it is the first sale doctrine (Section 109 Copyright Act) that rules. According to that, once the artist transfers title of his work his or her rights to any further compensation are exhausted.

---

68 Merryman 1992, pp. 107–108.

69 Werbin 2014.

70 California Civil Code § 986 (c)(1).

71 California Civil Code § 986 (a).

72 California Civil Code § 986 (a)(7). See also Kumar 2014, p. 448.

73 *Estate of Graham v. Sotheby's Inc.*, 860 F. Supp. 2d 1117 (C.D. Cal. 2012).

74 O'Donnell 2014a.

75 O'Donnell 2014b.

76 Rub 2014, p. 3.

77 Rub 2013, p. 133.

The actual argument in favor of such a law enactment is that there is discrimination in U.S. copyright law against visual artists.[78] It is also supported that royalty rights would encourage artists to be more prolific and help expand secondary markets. Furthermore, reciprocity with foreign resale royalty rules would produce new foreign revenue for American artists, it is argued.

The opponents to such a regulation argue that there are significant costs to resale royalties[79] and that in case of enactment they would not increase the total income of visual artists but they would redistribute some of it in favor of successful artists, something undesirable, according to a certain opinion, since successful artists do not value extra income as much as less successful ones do.[80] Furthermore, they fear of the secondary market fleeing from the U.S. to countries like China and Switzerland which provide no resale royalties.

In 2011, a representative introduced at the federal level a *droit de suite* bill.[81] That bill attracted no co-sponsors.

The same Representative re-introduced a new resale royalty bill on February 2014.[82] This is much broader that the previous one. It would cover artists who (i) are citizens of or domiciled either in the U.S. or a country that provides resale royalty rights; or (ii) have first created the work in the U.S. or a country that provides such royalty rights.

This bill has garnered multiple co-sponsors and on July 15, 2014 a further Congressional hearing took place. Although there are positive comments, there are still strong opponents and the outcome is not yet foreseeable.

No such right is being recognized by the Swiss law.

References

Applebaum JR (1992) The visual artists rights act of 1990: an analysis based on the French droit moral. Am J Int Law Policy 8:183–223

Barron A (2002) Copyright law and the claims of art. Intellect Prop Q 4:368–401

Bock EM (2011) Using public disclosure as the vesting point for moral rights under the visual artists rights act. Mich Law Rev 110:153–174

Bonneau SG (2013) Honor and destruction: the conflicted object in moral rights law. St. John's Law Rev 87:47–105

Brauneis R (2013) National treatment in copyright and related rights: how much work does it do? The George Washington Law School Public Law and Legal Theory Paper No. 2013-103. http://ssrn.com/abstract=2291630

[78] Perlmutter 1992, p. 403.

[79] Hansmann and Santilli 2001, p. 259.

[80] Landes and Posner 1989, p. 327.

[81] The representative *J. Nadler* introduced the: H.R. 3688, "Equity for Visual Artists Act of 2011".

[82] H.R. 4103, "American Royalties Too Act of 2014".

Butera A (2010) A seemingly small, but major victory for visual artists. NYSBA Entertain, Arts Sports Law J 21:125–129
Corbett S (2012a) The digital museum and copyright law: can there be reconciliation? New Zealand Intellect Prop J 6:882–887
Corbett S (2012b) Maori cultural heritage and copyright law: a balancing exercise. New Zealand Intellect Prop J 6:916–921
Costonis J (2000) Casting light on cultural property (book review). Mich Law Rev 98:1837–1862
Cotter TF (1997) Pragmatism, economics, and the droit moral. North Carolina Law Rev 76:1–97
Dietz A (1995) The moral right of the author: moral rights and the civil law countries. Columbia-VLA J Law Arts 19:199–228
Dine JM (1995) Authors' moral rights in non-european nations: international agreements, economics, Mannu Bhandari, and the Dead Sea Scrolls. Mich J Int Law 16:545–583
Dworkin G (1995) The moral right of the author: moral rights and the common law countries. Columbia-VLA J Law Arts 19:229–267
Farley CH (2005) Judging art. Tulane Law Rev 79:805–858
Favretto S (2007) Il diritto a braccetto con l'arte. Opportunita e tutele giuridiche nei beni culturali e paesaggistici, nel mercato delle opera d'arte. Edizioni Falsopiano, Alessandria
Fenzel C (2007) Still life with "spark" and "sweat": the copyrightability of contemporary art in the United States and the United Kingdom. Ariz J Int Comp Law 24:541–585
Ginsburg JC (2003) The concept of authorship in comparative copyright law. DePaul Law Rev 52:1063–1092
Ginsburg JC (2005) The author's name as a trademark: a perverse perspective on the moral right of "paternity"? Cardozo Arts Entertain Law J 23:379–389
Gover KE (2012) Christoph Büchel v. mass MoCA: a tilted arc for the twenty-first century. J Aesthetic Educ 46:46–58. doi:10.5406/jaestdeuc.46.1.0046
Hansmann H, Santilli M (2001) Royalties for artists versus royalties for authors and composers. J Cult Econ 25:259–281
Heymann LA (2005) The birth of the authornym: authorship, pseudonymity, and trademark law. Notre Dame Law Rev 80:1377–1449
Hudson E (2006) Cultural institutions, law and indigenous knowledge: a legal primer on the management of Australian indigenous collections. University of Melbourne, Intellectual Property Research Institute of Australia
Janke T (2005) Managing indigenous knowledge and indigenous cultural and intellectual property, In: Nakata M, Langton M (eds) Australian indigenous knowledge and libraries. Australian Academic and Research Libraries, 36(2):95–107. doi: 10.1080/00048623.2005.10721251
Kumar N (2014) Constitutional hazard: The California resale royalty act and the futility of state-level implementation of droit de suite legislation. Columbia J Law Arts 37:443–462
Kwall RR (2001) Preserving personality and reputational interests of constructed personas through moral rights: a blueprint for the twenty-first century. Univ Ill Law Rev 151–172
Ladas SP (1938) The international protection of literary and artistic property. The Macmillan Co, New York
Landes WE, Posner RA (1989) An economic analysis of copyright law. J Legal Stud 18:325–363
Liemer SP (1998) Understanding artists' moral rights: a primer. Boston Univ Public Interest Law J 7:41-57
Liemer SP (2005) How we lost our moral rights and the door closed on non-economic values in copyright. John Marshall Rev Intellect Prop Law 5:1–37
Loughlan P (2002) The ravages of public use: aboriginal art and moral rights. Media Arts Law Rev 7:17–26
Merryman JH (1976) The refrigerator of bernard buffet. Hastings Law J 27:1023–1049
Merryman JH (1992) The wrath of Robert Rauschenberg. Am J Comp Law 41:103–127
Moore AD (2003) Intellectual property, innovation, and social progress: the case against incentive based arguments. Hamline Law Rev 26:601–630
Munzer SR, Raustiala K (2009) The uneasy case for intellectual property rights in traditional knowledge. Cardozo Arts Entertain Law J 27:37–97

Ng A (2009) The social contract and authorship, allocating entitlements in the copyright system. Fordham Intellect Prop Media Entertain Law J 19:413–482
O'Donnell N (2014a) Have some foie gras with your ethanol: auction houses urge ninth circuit not to rehear California resale royalties act argument. The art law report. http://www.artlawreport.com/2014/09/23/have-some-foie-gras-with-your-ethanol-auction-houses-urge-ninth-circuit-not-to-rehear-california-resale-royalties-act-arguments/
O'Donnell N (2014b) Full ninth circuit to review california resale royalty act en banc. The art law report. http://www.artlawreport.com/2014/10/31/full-ninth-circuit-to-revie-california-resale-royalty-act-en-banc/
Perlmutter S (1992) Resale royalties for artists: an analysis of the register of copyrights' report. Columbia-VLA J Law Arts 16:395–425
Plaisant R (1987) Droit de suite and droit moral under the berne convention. Columbia-VLA J Law Arts 11:157–164
Price ME (1968) Government policy and economic security for artists: the case of the droit de suite. Yale Law J 77:1333–1366
Prowda JB (2013) Visual arts and the law. a handbook for professionals, Lund Humphries in association with Sotheby's Institute of Art, Farnham
Rector SL (2010) A training ground for contemporary art: massachusetts museum of contemporary art v. Büchel's overly broad exclusion of artistic collaborations. Univ Colorado Law Rev 81:581–626
Redish MH (2005) Summary judgment and the vanishing trial: implications of the litigation matrix. Stanf Law Rev 57:1329–1359
Rigamonti CP (2006) Deconstructing moral rights. Harv Int Law J 47:353–412
Rigamonti CP (2007) The conceptual transformation of moral rights. Am J Comp Law 55:67–122
Roeder MA (1940) The doctrine of moral right: a study in the law of artists, authors, and creators. Harv Law Rev 53:554–578
Rozell M (2014) The art collector's handbook. a guide to collection management and care. Lund Humphries in association with Sotheby's Institute of Art, Farnham
Rub GA (2013) Stranger than kryptonite: inalienable profit sharing schemes in copyright law. Harv J Law Technol 27:49–133
Rub GA (2014) The unconvincing case for resale royalties. Yale Law J Forum 124:1–10. http://www.yalelawjournal.com/forum/the-unconvincing-case-for-resale-royalties
Sax JL (1999) Playing darts with a rembrandt. public and private rights in cultural treasures. The University of Michigan Press, Ann Arbor
Sobre el estatuto jurídico tributario del coleccionista en España y posibles medidas que contribuyan a su promoción (2014) Informe de la Fundación Arte y Mecenazgo, Barcelona
Tang X (2012) The artist as brand: toward a trademark conception of moral rights. Yale Law J 122:218–257
Telesetsky A (2008) Massachusetts museum of contemporary art foundation, inc. v. Christoph Büchel, U.S. District of Massachusetts, Case 3:07-cv-30089-MAP. Int J Cult Prop 15:87–95
Telesetsky A (2011) Massachusetts museum of contemporary art foundation v. Christoph Büchel: an appellate perspective on the visual artists rights act. Int J Cult Prop 18:255–258
Tipton S (2009) Connoisseurship corrected: protecting the artist, the public and the role of art museums through the amendment of VARA. Rutgers Law Rev 62:269–303
Tischler RJ (2012) "The power to tax involves the power to destroy". How avant-garde art outstrips the imagination of regulators, and why a judicial rubric can save it. Brooklyn Law Rev 77:1665–1705
Tushnet R (2012) Worth a thousand words: the images of copyright. Harv Law Rev 125:683–759
Werbin B (2014) Federal art resale royalty inches toward reality. art and advocacy 18
Wu LF (2009) Museum of contemporary art v. Büchel: construing artists' rights in the context of institutional commissions. Columbia J Law Arts 32:151–178

Chapter 4
Comparative Approaches to the Study of National Museums

4.1 General Comments

Difference in all its forms—cultural, temporal, geographical, and physical—is a central issue[1] in museums [too] regardless of their nature—ethnographic, historical, artistic, archaeological, or scientific.[2] Museums' settings are different, because each one of them is formed in a specific society,[3] in a specific culture.[4]

"Why are there national museums all over the world?", asks Peter Aronsson. What are their differences and their similarities? He refers to MacGregor, according to whom, "the first expansion of the concept of the museum occurred in the shift from early modern aristocratic treasury museums to cabinets of curiosities, which moved attention from the representation of splendor to the possibilities of a space of enquiry".

The formation of nation-states at about the end of the 18th century and the beginning of the 19th century is the turning point for the [national] museums too.[5]

A particularly interesting "contradiction" is that "although the museum was introduced around the world as a result of colonialism and international relations

---

[1] "…, difference always shadows and doubles identity, always entails a relationship between self and other.", see Sherman 2008, p. 1.

[2] Dias 2008, p. 124.

[3] Drengwitz and Elbers and Jahn and Wrogemann 2014, p. 98.

[4] See McClellan 2008b, p. 25: "Needless to say, it is precisely the flattening of difference – differences of culture, class, and definitions of art across space and time – in a reductive pursuit if essential identities that recent critics of the museum have sought to explode as so many myths designed to occlude the power relations between peoples and between institutions and their publics".

[5] Aronsson 2008, p. 11. He points out that the "successive spread of the [cabinet of curiosity] model went, on a macro-historical scale and in accordance with regular models of colonialism and globalization, almost simultaneously to the white colonies in Charleston (1773), Rio de Janeiro (1815), Sydney (1821), Cape Town (1825)".

E. Moustaira, *Art Collections, Private and Public: A Comparative Legal Study*, SpringerBriefs in Law, DOI 10.1007/978-3-319-15802-0_4

(trade, diplomatic visits, emulation, and so on),[6] the first global boom in *national* museum took place in the decades after 1870, at the high tide of imperial expansionism with a second wave taking place during a phase of post-colonial nationalism after the Second World War".[7]

And of course this is true, since the museums and, accordingly, the expositions at first were invented for objects of occidental cultures. Afterwards, and especially during the 19th century, when colonial and military expeditions were at their peak and archaeological excavations were multiplied, museums started (or continued) collecting non-Western artifacts. Preservation of material culture was the "excuse" Western museums were almost steadily invoking, presenting themselves as the most suitable for that absolutely necessary procedure.[8]

Later, things changed slightly and the museums, as institutions of "Western invention",[9] were exported to or implanted in other places, other countries, former colonies of occidental countries. At the beginning, they were mostly in disposal of the administrative and commercial colonial high officials, as a means of education and recreation at the same time.[10] It is with reason argued that in the past but also at present, "wherever they have taken root they conform essentially to the Western model in their core ideals, taxonomic principles, and administrative structure".[11]

Many are the intellectuals and the artists who have opposed to the idea and the existence of the museums. Common ground of all those people's ideas was and is their belief in an art that has a specific destination, a moral or theological value.[12]

Even museologists recognize sometimes that the museum, regarding the art work's birth, is an imposition. As it is stated: "we could support the awkward opinion that in reality no art work was ever born to be placed in a museum and [by saying that] we would not be very far from the truth".[13]

---

[6] Craik 2007, p. 37.

[7] Aronsson 2011, pp. 30–31.

[8] See Balachandran 2007, pp. 8–9, commenting on the looting and collecting of Chinese art objects by mosty Euro-Americans and on the arguments that Western museums were successively in time using for appropriating them, in order to "preserve" them: "First, they were identified as scientific institutions with specialists capable of properly cataloging, studying, and analyzing the material. Next, they were proposed as safe and secure repositories for artifacts. Finally, it was assumed that artifacts could be better appreciated for their intrinsic artistic, cultural, and historic significance by Western museum audiences rather than in their home countries where they were little valued".

[9] It is an institution based on the principles of the Enlightenment, the program of which, in regard of art, was to render it public, contrary to what was happening until then with the royal collections. Ever since then, one can no more define the people who visit museums, they are no more a community of people with an sacred art axis, see Moustaira 2007, p. 387.

[10] This is one of the reasons for which most of the objects presented in museums and expositions had not been created to be exposed. It is a "forced spectacularisation" of objects withdrawn from their context, see Rossignol 2009, p. 30.

[11] McClellan 2008a, p. 5.

[12] Déotte 2001, p. 14.

[13] Strinati 2008, p. 11.

According to that point of view, a museum does not constitute a place of memory for the human communities, it only presents objects of those communities to an indefinite public, to individualities that may be rendered aesthetic subjectivities due to their "meeting" with certain of those objects presented in a museum. Art, it is argued, is the realization of truth[14] and this truth is presented through the space, the place of an art work.[15] However, the uniform way of presenting artworks in a museum places them on the same level.[16]

Others argue differently. They believe—and obviously they express Western ideas—that the museum is this tool that invents art as a modern concept of aesthetics. They argue that such tools, as the museum, are those that give a basis of presentation to the arts and impose on them their laic power, the definition that those give to the common sensibility.[17]

As it is pointed out in a study of national museums—but the observation is valid on an international level –, a juridical analysis of the museums is particularly complex because of the fact that the museums do not constitute a homogeneous reality. There are art museums, archaeological museums, science museums, ethnographic museums, history museums, natural museums, specialized (numismatic, industrial, etc.) museums. There are also State museums, regional museums, provincial museums, university museums, ecclesiastical museums, etc.[18]

A systematic [not only legal] comparison of national museums could be done for various reasons. Some have the ambition to formulate a single theoretical statement, by reaching general conclusions about the process of creation of national museums and their functions. Somewhat on the contrary, others try to connect strategies for the development of national museums to the birth and development of the nation states, nuancing thus generalizations about national museums.

Other reasons for such a systematic comparison could be the need to find out the exact role of the museums in a national system, the uniqueness of those museums, or "simply" to develop new questions about "the object under scrutiny", that is, the national museums.[19]

In any case, it is very interesting to study "the parallel interactions between museum, nation and state and give witness to the long standing relevance of national museums as constituent components of… negotiated cultural constitutions

[14] See Heidegger 2003 (1960), p. 30: "Im Werk der Kunst hat sich die Wahrheit des Seienden ins Werk gesetzt".

[15] Marion 2007, p. 60.

[16] Heidegger 2003 (1960), p. 35: "So stehen und hängen denn die Werke selbst in den Sammlungen und Ausstellungen. Aber sind sie hier an sich als die Werke, die sie selbst sind, oder sind sie eher als die Gegenstände des Kunstbetriebes?".

[17] Puelles Romero 2011, p. 61, notes that the Museum and the Art Critique are two realms of knowledge and of sensibility that were borne in the 18th century and that during the posterior centuries acted and continue to act as institutional representatives of knowledge and power, as two factors that intervene in the modeling of the spectators′ sensibility.

[18] Morbidelli 2010, p. 5.

[19] Aronsson 2008, pp. 8–9.

through which nations express their yearning for a golden and legitimate past, balancing perceived needs for continuity with increasing diversity and difference of present circumstances in which a unified agenda of the future may be challenged".[20]

So, according to the above idea, a unitary ideal of national museum is best represented in strong centralized states. There are such museums in Finland, Denmark, Wales and Hungary.

Another interesting historical observation is that in the past, the Soviet influence on Eastern Europe's cultural policy had supported centralization. Thus, in those countries—Lithuania, Hungary, Bulgaria, Romania, the former Czechoslovakia and the former Yugoslavia—Marxism had "used" national museums for purposes of organizational and narrative unity.[21]

4.2 National Museums' Characteristics: Are There?

In Portugal, the general principles of the Museums Act ("Lei-Quadro-dos Museos Portugueses") are, as stated[22]:

- The principle of person's primacy (Article 2 para 1a): a person's access to cultural objects is absolutely necessary for his/her fulfillment.
- The principle of promoting responsible citizenship (Article 2 para 1b): all citizens are encouraged to be engaged in the safeguard, enrichment and promotion of museums, "as keepers of cultural property". This is in alignment with the fundamental right to cultural enjoyment and creation that Article 78 of the Portuguese Constitution has established.
- The principle of public service (Article 2 para 1c): cultural objects have a strong legal-social value. The museums cannot use them for selfish reasons, since they —museums—exist in order to serve the community. It is most interesting that this principle also covers private museums.
- The principle of coordination (Article 2 para 1d): it requires the articulation of guidelines for the structuring of museums, which must be coordinated with the guidelines of other, connected to cultural property, domains, that is, education, science, territorial planning, environment and tourism.
- The principle of transversality (Article 2 para 1e): the same treatment is guaranteed to all cultural objects, regardless of their institutional ownership, origin or nature.
- The principle of information (Article 2 para 1f): the widest possible dissemination of knowledge, nationally and internationally, about museums and cultural heritage must be allowed.

---

[20] Aronsson and Elgenius 2011, pp. 5–6.

[21] Aronsson and Elgenius 2011, pp. 15–16.

[22] Laureano 2014, p. 49.

- The principle of supervision (Article 2 para 1g): the State has the duties of "identification and incentive of procedures that constitute good museum practices, of initiatives promoting qualification and good functioning of museums and of measures preventing the destruction, loss or damage of cultural assets embedded in them".
- The principle of decentralization (Article 2 para1h): municipal museums and their role in the access of culture are valorized.
- The principle of international cooperation (Article 2 para 1i): an international exchange of efforts and experiences must be favored.

In Spain, the laws on museums—those of the State and those of the Comunidades Autónomas[23]—provide that the public authorities (and the museums are such public authorities) must guarantee the citizens' access to culture. This is one of the duties of the museums together with the guarantee of the conservation of the historical patrimony and of its enrichment.

These two principles, as far as the acting of the public authorities on the subject of cultural and historical patrimony is concerned, are contained in the Spanish Constitution.[24]

In France, the museum has been always constructed around the notion of public service or of the service to the public.[25] This is clearly confirmed also by the law of 4.1.2002 which consecrates the basic principles that are the foundation of the museum's existence: the collections' conservation and their presentation to the public.[26]

4.3 Indigenous Communities and National Museums

In several parts of the world, not only persons are encouraged to participate in the life of museums, but also the communities as such. This is one of the aims of the Latin American New Museology. One basic reason for this was and is the need to value the cultural patrimony of the marginal communities as a strategy of affirmative visibility, which will give them the stand to ask for rights.

As it is rightly argued, the cultural recognition of the various communities is fundamental for their self-esteem. For this to happen, the communities must have an active role, even a protagonist role, in the management of the cultural patrimony. This is important, it is argued, for the sustainability of museums in Latin America. Inviting the communities to work together with museum specialists in order to determine the various patrimonies or the way to exhibit them would be the proper

[23] See infra, 6.5.

[24] Stampa 2007, p. 21.

[25] Fumaroli 1994, p. 5.

[26] Fatôme 1994, p. 15.

manner to resolve the problem of irreconcilability between communities and museums.

This is not easy to happen, though, it is admitted. From the about 6 thousand museums that there are in Latin America more than the 80 % do not have the necessary conditions to efficiently execute their mission.[27]

Furthermore, one of the subjects of the heated discussions of recent years about the respect that should be paid to the cultural sovereignty of the indigenous peoples, namely their sovereignty over their cultural heritage, tangible and intangible, is also the expediency of foundation of museums exclusively dedicated to these cultures. Would such an institutional frame be necessary?[28]

The answer will be yes if we realize that museums constitute educational tools and that museum expositions can create narratives on the world and its people.[29] These educational tools can be used to create and eternalize ideologies and historical memories.[30] Museum curators, by exposing museum objects in a certain way, become history's interpreters.[31]

In USA, Native Americans and the objects related to them were almost always treated as exotic curiosities.[32] The emergence of the anthropology at about the end of the 19th century and beginning of the 20th century gave a new perspective to the treatment of those people. However, even then it did not manage to revert the reigning mentality.

The development of the new tribal museums in USA started after 1960, was especially developed after 1970 and then again after 1990. Contrary to the fears expressed that these museums would replace traditional institutions, they have fortified those institutions.

Since the beginning, they collected, preserved, and interpreted objects for their communities. Furthermore, they proceeded to historic research and they helped to the maintenance of the native languages.[33] One reason for their development was, on the one hand the reaction to the imperialistic activity of foreign museums which collect and interpret the Native American's culture and on the other hand their will to become the central axis of the tribal communities' emergence.[34]

---

27 Yudice 2010, pp. 32–33.

28 Moustaira 2012, p. 71.

29 Moser 2010, p. 22.

30 Vicenti Carpio 2006, p. 620.

31 Tsosie 2009, p. 3.

32 King 2009, p. 25.

33 According to Shyllon 2009, p. 159, the foundation of museums in Africa could have impeded or diminished the "whole-sale" removal of cultural objects from the colonies to the Western metropolises.

34 King 2009, p. 25.

4.4 Differences Between Museums of European Countries and Museums of the North American Countries

According to one opinion, in order to understand how the actual economic crisis affects the museums' world, it is very important to understand that the founding myths, the social role and the structures for the financing of museums of European countries are very different from those of the North American countries. Accordingly, the proposed solutions must correspond to the values and models of each and every one.[35]

In European countries, during the 19th century but also later, the museum was a formative element of the patriotic sentiment, a wake-up alarm of the national conscience, a catalyst of national art.

According to a Spanish scholar of the 19th century—speaking about Museo del Prado—the museums of the nations were not being constructed nor sustained by the Aerarium only in order for the students or the amateurs to do their exercise by copying statues or paintings. There was an even higher human and patriotic aim: to signal the milestones of the human work and the national culture.[36]

The evolution of museums in North America took a different path from that of the European countries' museums. The national museums in the American continent are first created at about the middle years of the 19th century, when the new States had already become independent. It is observed that the first national collections are those of natural sciences: geological, botanical, zoological, etc. This fact testifies that the national governments were trying to make inventories of the natural resources of their countries.

Today, museums in USA can have three basic forms. First, they may be charitable trusts, if they are formed under the terms of a person's trust instrument. An example of this form is the Barnes Museum in Pennsylvania. Second, they may incorporate under the rules of a state law for a not-for-profit incorporation. Third, they may be operated by the government.[37]

In Canada, William Edmond Logan and the scientists of the Geologic Commission of Canada had already in 1842 prepared an inventory of natural resources and also gathered specimens of natural sciences. These collections were the basis of the first national museum of Canada, in Montreal.

---

35 Bergeron 2009–2010, p. 60.

36 "No se erigen, no deben erigirse los museos de las naciones, ni sostenerse por el Erario, únicamente para que el alumno o el aficionado utilice lienzos y estatuas ejercitándose en copiarlas. Con ser este fin muy legítimo, tiene el Museo, desde luego, otro más elevado, humano y patriótico: el señalar los términos por donde llegó el trabajo del hombre y la cultura nacional, en una faz principalísima, a la decadencia o prosperidad en que se la contempla siendo este raciocinio exacto, el Museo se halla incluido dentro de la órbita de las instituciones docentes, cuya existencia interesa a todos y cada uno de los españoles", F.M. Tubino, Crítica artística. El Museo del Prado, La Academia de Bellas Artes y el catálogo del señor Madrazo, Revista de España 1872, pp. 513–514: it is referred by Gutiérrez Burón 2013, p. 189.

37 Fincham 2011, p. 9.

What is very interesting is that the country's exploration also led the scientists to gather objects that would be testimonies of the life of indigenous in America. This is the reason why the ethnographic collections in America only appear at the second half of the 19th century while in Europe museums conserve Amerindian collections since the time of the discovery and exploration of America, in the 16th century.[38]

During the second half of the 19th century, many museums are created, dedicated to the history and ethnology. Given the fact that all of the countries had been colonies in the past, they wanted to valorize their national history and take a distance from the European countries that had colonized them.

In Canada, one observes a real development of museums especially during the celebrations for the 100 years of the Confederation, in 1967. The federal government and the provincial governments establish a net of modern museums sharing the same mentality as those of USA.

A very important characteristic of Canada, and an important difference between this country and USA, is that the federal government gives priority to the multicultural politics. This is the reason why Canadian museums have and conserve objects that are considered as testimonies of the various cultural communities which contributed to the formation of a country such as Canada.

As far as the museums' collections are concerned, it is observed that contrary to what happens in the big USA museums, the museums of Quebec do not have important Amerindian collections.

A part of the national collection which is now conserved in the Museum of Civilization had been gathered by the priests of the "Séminaire de Québec", foundational institution of the first French colony in America. Nevertheless, the majority of the items of this national collection were gathered during the second half of the 20th century.[39]

As far as the Séminaire de Québec's collections are concerned, it is mentioned that it was its double filiation, on the one hand to its French origins and on the other hand to the Canadian specificity, which was "responsible" for the richness of its collections, able to construct a national project, and perhaps for the slight importance that was given to the Amerindians' cultural treasures.

In the 19th century there had been created in Quebec geological, mineralogical and numismatic collections, dispersed in thematic museums. When in 1952 the Séminaire de Québec created the Université Laval, the first catholic francophone institution de superior education Bas-Canada, these collections were officially put in the service of the University studies. This University's museum, due to the ancient and original items of its collections was considered as the «berceau de l'Amérique française».[40]

---

[38] Bergeron 2009–2010, p. 60.

[39] Renier 2013, p. 121.

[40] Renier 2013, p. 122.

References

Aronsson P (2008) Comparing national museums: methodological reflections. In: Aronsson P, Nyblom A (eds) NaMu IV, comparing: national museums, territories, nation-building and change. Linköping University, Norrköping, pp 11–19. http://www.ep.liu.se/ecp/030/

Aronsson P (2011) Explaining national museums: exploring comparative approaches to the study of national museums. In: Knell SJ, Aronsson P, Amundsen AB, Barnes AJ, Burch S, Carter J, Gosselin V, Hughes SA, Kirwan A (eds) National museums: new studies from around the world. Routledge, London, pp 29–54

Aronsson P, Elgenius G (2011) Making national museums in Europe—a comparative approach. In: Aronsson P, Elgenius G (eds) Building national museums in Europe 1750-2010, conference proceedings from EuNaMus, European national museums: identity politics, the uses of the past and the European citizen. Linköping University, Bologna, 28–30 April 2011, pp 5–20. http://www.ep.liu.se/ecp_home/index.en.aspx?issue=064

Balachandran S (2007) Object lessons: the politics of preservation and museum building in Western China in the early twentieth century. Int J Cult Prop 14:1–32

Bergeron Y (2009–2010) Los museos y la crisis. Tendencias en los museos norteamericanos. Revista Museos 5(6):58–67

Craik J (2007) Re-visioning arts and cultural policy. current impasses and future directions. The Australian National University E Press, Canberra. http://epress.anu.edu.au/revisioning_citation.html

Déotte J-L (2001) Le musée de l'Europe à l'épreuve de la disparition. Tumultes 16:13–27

Dias N (2008) cultural difference and cultural diversity. The case of the Musée du Quai Branly. In: Sherman DJ (ed) Museums and difference. Indiana University Press, Bloomington, pp 124–154

Drengwitz B, Elbers B, Jahn LD, Wrogemann I (2014) Nation and national museums, a contested relationship: an analysis of U.S. national museums in the twenty-first century, Curator Museum J 57:97–106

Fatôme E (1994) Les musées et l'idée de service public. In: Bonnefous E, Peuchot E, Richer L (dir) Droit au musée, droit des musées. Dalloz, Paris, pp 15–42

Fincham D (2011) Deaccession of art from the public trust. Art Antiq Law 16:1–37

Fumaroli M (1994) Les musées au service du public, les origines. In: Bonnefous E, Peuchot E, Richer L (dir) Droit au musée, droit des musées. Dalloz, Paris, pp 5–13

Gutiérrez Burón J (2013) Las adquisiciones oficiales en las exposiciones nacionales de bellas artes en el siglo XIX. In: Socias I, Gkozgkou D (eds) Nuevas contribuciones en torno al mundo del coleccionismo de arte hispánico en los siglos XIX y XX. Ediciones Trea, Gijón (Asturias), pp 173–192

Heidegger M (2003[1960]) Der Ursprung des Kunstwerkes. Reclam, Stuttgart

King DH (2009) Exhibiting culture: american indians and museums. Tulsa Law Rev 45:25–32

Laureano A (2014) A brief survey on some essentials of Portuguese museum law. Revista Museologia e Patrimônio 7:3–20

Marion E (2007) Phénoménologie de l'art: Le site de l'œuvre, la place de la collection. Museum Int 235:57–65

McClellan A (2008a) The art museum from Boullée to Bilbao. University of California Press, Berkeley

McClellan A (2008b) Art museums and commonality. a history of high ideals. In: Sherman DJ (ed) Museums and Difference. Indiana University Press, Bloomington, pp 25–59

Morbidelli G (2010) Introduzione. In: Morbidelli G, Cerrina Feroni G (a cura di) I musei. Discipline, gestioni, prospettive. G. Giappichelli Editore, Torino, pp 3–21

Moser S (2010) The devil is in the detail: museums displays and the creation of knowledge. Museum Anthropol 33:22–32

Moustaira EN (2007) Book review. Revue Hellénique de Droit International 60:387–391

Moustaira EN (2012) Comparative law and cultural objects [in Greek]. Nomiki Vivliothiki, Athens

Puelles Romero L (2011) Mirar al que mira. Teoría estética y sujeto espectador. ABADA EDITORES, Madrid

Renier M (2013) Entre France et Amérique, la mise en valeur d'un patrimoine amérindien au séminaire de Québec. In: Bergeron Y, Frey V (dir) Archives et musées. Le théâtre du patrimoine (France-Canada). Editions du Comité des travaux historiques et scientifiques, pp 121–136

Rossignol C (2009) L'exposition comme source d'illusions d'optique culturelles. In: Somé R, Schutz C (dir) Anthropologie, art contemporain et musée: Quels liens? L'Harmattan, Paris, pp 29–38

Sherman DJ (2008) Introduction. In: Sherman DJ (ed) Museums and Difference. Indiana University Press, Bloomington, pp 1–21

Shyllon F (2009) Unraveling history: return of African cultural objects repatriated and looted in colonial times. In: Nafziger JAR, Nicgorski AM (eds) Cultural heritage issues: the legacy of conquest, colonization, and commerce. Martinus Nijhoff Publishers, Leiden, pp 159–168

Stampa A (2007) Modelos de los museos. Panorama legal. Museo 12:19–32

Strinati C (2008) Il tema. In: Calvano T, Di Monte MG, Mangia P (a cura di) Museo tra passato e presente. Meltemi editore, Roma, pp 9–13

Tsosie R (2009) Native nations and museums: developing an institutional framework for cultural sovereignty. Tulsa Law Rev 45:3–24

Vicenti Carpio M (2006) (Un)disturbing exhibitions: indigenous historical memory at the NMAI. American Indian Quarterly 30:619–631

Yudice G (2010) Museu Molecular e Desenvolvimento Cultural? In: Do Nascimento Junior J (org.), Economia de museus. Brasilia, Ministerio da Cultura; Instituto Brasileiro de Museus, pp 21–25

Chapter 5
Private Collections "Versus" Public Collections

5.1 General Comments

This relation has two "faces": private collections wishing to become somehow more open to the public, or/and public collections receding, leaving (willingly or unwillingly) space to the private participation.

Having in mind that collecting is often idiosyncratic, one wonders which are the principal factors of divergence, in order that collecting acquires an institutional character.

According to one opinion, the true collections are necessarily private, since they have the signature of the personal preferences of the collectors. Would such a "reading" be verified today?

The public access and the musealization of the private collections are becoming determinant factors. What are the reasons that make a collector give up on his or her right of exclusive usufruct of his or her cultural objects and share them with the public? Philanthropy, social prestige, fiscal benefits, the idea of the collection's continuity with the name of the collector linked to a public institution? And what are the contemporary tendencies in the field of private collecting[1]?

In these parts of Europe where the State does not give enough money to the art museums, private collections have acquired "almost without a fight" an increasing power during the first decade of the 21st century.[2]

In Switzerland, since several decades ago has been established a sort of collaboration between public museums, big collectors' families and new financially powerful private institutions. In France, on the one hand there is always a big budget available to the public institutions for buying art works and on the other hand there is the right of museums to buy first in case of auctions or heritages following the death of important artists.

[1] Duarte 2013, p. 19.
[2] Fleck 2013, p. 69.

E. Moustaira, *Art Collections, Private and Public: A Comparative Legal Study*, SpringerBriefs in Law, DOI 10.1007/978-3-319-15802-0_5

The new geography of art collecting has been transformed and new regions are at the front lately. Thus, we are informed about collectors from China, Southeast Asia, Middle East, or Indian subcontinent. It is stated that in these regions there is not an international network of public museums but there is some sort of connection between private institutions on the one side and official state collections on the other side.[3]

Concerning the most important issue of art restoration's and conservation's techniques, it is proposed that a public museum could provide assistance to galleries and collectors on the correct treatment of art objects, especially when they are too many and too different as far as their needs are concerned.

According to this very interesting opinion, the public institutions have a central role for the future, since it is those that on the one hand have the necessary infrastructure, and on the other hand have to apply the international protocols of art objects' conservation. As it is pointed out, the whole subject of restoration and correct conservation of the cultural objects is very important to the cycle of private collectors who often undervalue it.[4]

5.2 Collaboration Between Museums and Collectors

5.2.1 Germany

Article 5 Abs. 3 S.1 of the German Constitution (*Grundgesetz*) guarantees the freedom of art. The reasons that this freedom has been guaranteed constitutionally, may be found in the need to correct errors of the totalitarian culture politics of the National Socialists. The same need to correct errors of the past, was also the reason for the multiple cooperation between public museums and private collectors during the years after the World War II.

As it is mentioned, during the 1980s there was a real boom of art museums in Germany.[5] Examples of museums that were founded at that time, are: in 1981 the Neue Pinakothek, in Munich, in 1982 the Abteiberg Museum in Mönchengladbach and the Staatsgalerie in Stuttgart, in 1986 the Kunstsammlung NRW in Düsseldorf.

At the beginning of 1990s, the German museums had to confront increasing costs, either in order to maintain the expensive museum buildings or to acquire contemporary art, the prices of which had gone up. The public sector was very reluctant to cover all these costs, especially the ones that were needed for the acquisition of new artworks. In order to be able to compensate for the lack of public means, many museums decided to work together with private collectors.

[3] Fleck 2013, pp. 72–74.

[4] Detheridge 2011, p. 33.

[5] Fischer 2012, p. 26.

In our days, contrary to what happens in the public museums which have a restricted budget for the acquisition of new artworks, there are many private collectors whose collections are becoming steadily bigger and richer. Their activities are being followed with much interest, for example many articles and books are written about them and their collections or by themselves.[6] Many of these private collectors work together with public museums while some other private collectors are not willing to do so.

The relations between public museums and private collectors are being variously judged by people. Some are very positive towards such a cooperation believing that the presentation of a private collection in a public museum gives the chance to the museum's visitors to be acquainted with artists that until the private collection's exhibition had not been discovered by the museum or that had been underestimated. Furthermore, private collectors supposedly have a better knowledge of specific sectors of contemporary art, while museums normally must cover a more general field, "loosing" therefore in details.

Those who are negative towards such a cooperation refer to the profit that collectors have by showing their collections in public museums, since normally the exposition of big collections in public spaces influences the art market and the collectors acquire economic and political power. It is also doubted, according to some opinion, that the items of private collections that are exposed in public museums may be "worth" such an exposition. Sometimes collectors buy items of contemporary art that can be considered as "correct" for an exhibition. These less important items may make sense in a private collection but their missing quality is too apparent when they are exposed together with the "masterworks" of a museum's collection.[7]

5.2.2 Contracts Between Museums and Collectors: Are They Governed by Public Law or Private Law?

The decision about this dilemma has many consequences. Especially for the culture sector, whether a contract will be governed by public or private law is linked to the question what sort of influence may the State have on the decisions about the support of the cultural life.[8]

At first, it should be mentioned that when the State is actively involved in the support of culture, it is not obliged to support all persons that would be considered as artists. On the contrary, the State is largely free to evaluate and decide whom it will support on the condition that not inadequate criteria are set as a basis for this

[6] One of the most famous German collectors who cooperated very fruitfully with various public museums is the businessman from Aachen, Peter Ludwig.

[7] Fischer 2012, pp. 30–31.

[8] Fischer 2012, p. 33.

choice.[9] It is argued that if the State had limitless freedom to choose whom to support among the artists, there would be a great danger of damaging the free art life and the State would be seen as having a role of "Art judge" (*Kunstrichter*).[10]

There is much discussion among German scholars on the above mentioned danger. It is argued that the classification of certain legal relationships in the realm of (State's responsibility) culture depends on whether these legal relationships have a controlling character by the administration or not. According to this opinion, this is what happens when museums buy art works.[11]

This stance is criticized by other scholars who point out that even in the far past there were doubts about the State organs' competence to take art decisions, due to the fear of abuse of such a competence.

Given the fact that there is not a specific juridical basis for the classification of the contracts between museums and collectors in the realm of public law or in the realm of private law,[12] the effort for such a classification has focused in the criteria that have been used by the case law and by legal theory.

Courts have supported the opinion that the classification of culture care as a State duty does not mean that contracts in the area of the not regulated by law culture care should be characterized as public law contracts. On the contrary, it is observed that the State, in the case of these contracts, may use private law instruments and this is exactly what happens especially in the case of museum expositions.

In praxis too, most if not all contracts between museums and collectors are concluded on the basis of private law rules—many of these contracts are loan contracts and they are regulated by §§ 598 ff of the German Civil Code (*Bundesgesetzbuch*). Also German scholars, researching about collectors, usually use as a model the private law contract.

In order to confirm that opinion, contracting between museums and collectors is compared to other means that museum uses for acquiring art works, objects of its activities, namely: collecting, researching, preserving and exposing. The most typical case is that of buying those artworks. This legal transaction, according to the dominant opinion, is a private law contract. It would at least be awkward, it is argued, to consider that case as a private law contract and at the same time characterize a time limited transfer, as an art work's loan is, as a public law contract.

Apparently the conclusion is that, at least in Germany, the contracts between museums and collectors, regarding the transfer of artworks, are private law contracts.[13]

---

[9] Fischer 2012, p. 34.

[10] Kadelbach 1997, p. 1117.

[11] Von Zezschwitz 1983, p. 1877.

[12] Fischer 2012, p. 36.

[13] Fischer 2012, pp. 40–41.

5.3 Public Access to Private Collections

The most usual problem is the access or rather the lack of access to a private collection.

The fact that a different mentality reigns in different legal cultures, as far as the role of [private or public] museums is concerned, that is, educational or keeper of national cultural heritage (see infra …), can up to a certain point explain the different stance that the national legislators keep.

Not everyone is happy with this situation, obviously. Jurists of a certain legal mentality tend to accuse foreign laws that treat this issue differently, for incoherence or incongruity. Read, for example, the following comment: "France, …, restricts the sale for export of works of art it considers part of its national patrimony, yet when a restricted work is then sold within France the new owner has no obligation to allow any form of public access to it".[14]

Various attitudes of national laws and private collectors residing in different jurisdictions might be traced.

A collector's voluntary attitude about allowing access to their collections, either to all people or to a restricted cycle of them, that is, artists, experts, and in general art connoisseurs, is considered as the best. Furthermore, this behavior does not need any legal regulation, if the access is informal. As it is very well depicted, "such practices can significantly bridge private and public imperatives".[15]

Beyond voluntary arrangements, there could be more options too, depending on the legal system: there are laws which try to "convince" private collectors to allow public access to their collections by using mostly tax incentives.

USA allows tax deductions for the value of gifts of art to public museums. United Kingdom offers on the one hand tax benefits to the collectors who sell or give artworks to the State or preserve them within national boundaries and on the other hand relief from certain capital taxes in exchange for which an owner of artworks may be obliged to make them available for public exhibition. Germany and Austria provide some relief from wealth taxes to those who gratuitously lend their collections to public museums for some years.

There are proposals for "a system of obligatory, expense-compensated loans to public institutions", admitting though that "implementing any such duty would be difficult, but my no means impossible".[16] These proposals have not been positively received by all. Except of the fact that such responsibilities would discourage collectors, as the opponents of these proposals very well stress out, it is difficult to say, whether such a system could be possible under every legal system.

---

[14] Sax 1999, p. 64.

[15] Sax 1999, p. 66.

[16] Sax 1999, pp. 66–67.

5.3.1 Private Collections Open to People—Converted to Public Collections

> Any private collection turned into a museum was bound to be a contradiction or at least a compromise. During the first great age of the collection museum, homes stood for inviolable privacy, whereas museums were quintessentially public. Museums even designated their audiences as a "public". Personal collection museums sought to balance opposites. Some never found that equilibrium; many lost it.[17]

Today, a proliferation of "private collector museums" has emerged, most notably in parts of the developing world where powerful collectors are employing their art to garner acceptance for global contemporary art or to educate the public on non-local movements in their respective regions. Other collectors share their collections more selectively on a very private basis.

New models of "public-private collections" continue to appear. They change the complexion of the art world.

As it is pointed out, sharing a collection with the public bestows social and cultural capital. By opening collections to the public, collectors assert their individual identity through their art, raise their public profile, and create a legacy. Collectors also gain market influence through their public spaces, establishing a greater position with dealers when it comes to acquisitions and possibly even raising the value of the art itself.

There are also tax benefits to be had in sharing collections.[18] And not always are the motives of the collectors completely clear. In some—if not many—cases, unfortunately, collectors try to cover the fact that the provenance of the collection's objects is not "known". Furthermore, often in these cases, collectors ask for a "reward", not at all insignificant.[19]

5.3.2 Donations by Private Collectors to Public Museums

A very common way for the public museums to enrich their collections is to accept donations by private persons, collectors or not. This way, museums may acquire artworks of great historic and aesthetic value.

In Spain, any acquisition in such a way of cultural goods needs the agreement of the Junta de Calificación, Valoración y Exportación de Bienes del PHE, as is the

---

[17] Higonnet 2010, p. 169.

[18] Rozell 2014, pp. 150–153.

[19] Such a case is commented by Lundén 2005. It is pointed out that the collector of rare—and many—manuscripts who had supposedly purchased them in Afghanistan in order to save them from the Talibans, was hoping that the collection would be purchased by thee Norwegian government for the National Library and placed in a new, special building. In 2003, he turned down an offer of over $110 million (800 million Norwegian korones). About this very big collection of scriptures "from all ages and places of the world", see also Matsuda 2000, p. 97.

rule for the contracts of the Public Administration. This *Junta* is an organ appointed to the Dirección General de Bellas Artes y Bienes Culturales.[20]

In United Kingdom, there are various examples of private collectors who donated their collection or parts of it to museums, while they were alive or after their death.

Such is the case of the late Sir Denis Mahon,[21] art connoisseur and collector, whose collection, under the terms of his will, has been given in perpetuity to six museums and galleries across Britain—to the National Gallery of Scotland in Edinburgh, to the National Gallery in London, to the Ashmolean in Oxford, to the Fitzwilliam in Cambridge, to the Birmingham Art Gallery, to Temple Newsam House in Leeds.

Under the terms of his will, if any of these museums and galleries ever decide to charge for admission, or if the attempt to sell any of their permanent collection, these donated works will have to be returned to the Art Fund, which is the independent national fundraising charity for art.[22]

The most recent example of such a donation is the controversial case of the "Gurlitt Collection". Many of the approximately 1,400 objects of the collection are of a shadowed origin, probably plundered during the years before the World War II by the Nazis.

These objects had disappeared for over a century and were "discovered" by the German police in the apartment of Cornelius Gurlitt, son of Hildebrandt Gurlitt's, a museum director who in 1933 was forced by the Nazis to resign but who, nevertheless, was one of the four dealers appointed by the Commission for the Exploitation of Degenerate Art ("Entartete Kunst") to sell confiscated and stolen artworks abroad.[23]

When Hildebrand Gurlitt died, the artworks of the collection passed down to his son, Cornelius, without the knowledge of the authorities. On February 28, 2012, the works were confiscated. There were and still are many legal problems about this collection. Claimants seeking restitution would face various problems, such as the German statute of limitations or the German laws of prescription.

Cornelius Gurlitt died in May 2014 and, 2 months after his death his testament was revealed in which he had made the Swiss Kunstmuseum Bern sole heir to his collection. The museum announced on November 24, 2014, at a conference with the German federal and the Bavarian governments, that it would accept the estate, insisting that it only will take possession of the artworks whose provenance is unproblematic. It remains to be seen what will happen in the future.

---

[20] Gonazález Sanz and Montero de Espinosa Helly 2011.

[21] He died at the age of 100 (1913–2013).

[22] Jardine 2013: "Whatever the case, as we stand in front of Guido Reni's exquisite painting The Rape of Europa in the National Gallery in London, marveling at the luminous colours and the studied elegance of the pose and draperies, we should reflect with a sense of gratitude—and a wry smile—on the determination of a single-minded individual like Sir Denis, who has ensured that any member of the public who wishes will always be able to share his pleasure free of charge".

[23] For many details about this case, see Amineddoleh 2014, p. 16.

5.4 Particular Collections: Spain—Thyssen-Bornemisza Collection

This collection comprises 787 paintings. The part of modern masters ("maestros modernos") comprises 338 paintings, all of them acquired after 1961, while the rest of it, that is the part of ancient masters ("maestros antiguos") was mostly inheritance of the previous Baron and only about 100 paintings acquired after 1961.[24]

By a law decree of 18 June of 1993 "Sobre medidas reguladoras del contrato de adquisición de la colección Thyssen-Bonremisza", the State has not bought the collection: it has given the money for the price to a foundation which was converted to owner of this collection. This is affirmed in the Article 2.2 which says: "...la colección propiedad de la Fundación y los cuadros integrantes de la misma no podrán ser objeto de enajenación, gravamen o embargo".

Probably because of the fact that it was a private foundation the one that acquired the collection and not the Spanish State, there was no intervention of the "Junta de Calificación, Valoración y Exportación de Bienes del Patrimonio Histórico Español", which should otherwise proceed to the evaluation of the paintings according to the Spanish legislation.

According to the Article 1.2, the State would pay the price for the collection's acquisition in five annuities of 8,455,424,000 pesetas each. Although it was not mentioned in the Law Decree, for the payment in five annuities, interest was foreseen.

It is very interesting that the contracts between the Spanish Administration and the Foundation for the payment, the cession of the seat, the financing of the differences between income and expenditure, are not governed by the Spanish law, as it is the rule for the State contracts, but by the English law.

By a recent Order of the Spanish Ministry of Culture (18.1.2011) the objects that are part of the "Contrato de Préstamo de Obras de Arte entre, de una parte, la Fundación Colección Thyssen-Bornemisza y, de otra Onicron Collections Limited, Nautilus Trustees Limited, Coraldale Navigation Incorporated, Imiberia Anstalt y la Baronesa Carmen Thyssen-Bornemisza" are guaranteed by the State. The value of the guaranteed objects (632: 625 paintings and other objects) was fixed in 41,578,881,366 euros. As it is pointed out, the fact that the State guarantees goods lent by various companies to a private foundation is really a surprise.[25]

---

[24] Cruz Valdovinos 2013, p. 90.

[25] Cruz Valdovinos 2013, p. 91.

5.5 Management of Private Collections

5.5.1 General Comments

"There are now more collectors worldwide than ever before", is declared, pointing out that "the digital age offers unprecedented ease of discovering and collecting art, bringing in more participants at every level".[26]

Sound art collection management starts at the acquisition stage.

Most collectors start buying art from an art dealer or art gallery—the first term is used in USA, while the second one is used in European countries, among others… Up until recently, most of the artworks were being sold by galleries, and it was be possible for a collector to be familiar with all of the art galleries in a certain place. Now, it is stated, big art markets such as London, New York, and Berlin have numerous galleries whose situations is not at all stable as markets boom and bust. Furthermore, usually nowadays, art is also being sold online.[27]

5.5.2 USA

More and more frequently, as a condition to having access to the most desirable artists, top galleries are requiring collectors to sign a right of first refusal at the time of purchase, meaning that if a collector wants to sell a work sometime in the future to a third party, he or she must offer it back to the original gallery at the same price before consigning or selling it.

If such an agreement is signed by the buyer, it will most likely be enforceable, although there are still few court cases to substantiate this. Most such claims settle out of court.

Courts often refer to a right of first refusal as a "pre-emptive right" because it allows the holder of the right to stop a sale that would otherwise take place.

The right of first refusal and other related rights (the right of "first consignment", the right of "first choice", prohibitions against sale) are not very common. … not every gallery with an artist in demand and a waiting list will impose the condition.[28]

In the case Robins V. Zwirner,[29] Robin claimed Zwirner verbally agreed to give Robins "first choice, after museums, to purchase one or more" of Dumas' works whenever Dumas had an exhibition at Zwirner's gallery …

---

[26] Rozell 2014, p.13. She mentions that some collectors, who possess large collections, employ entire art departments consisting of curators, collection managers, registrars and other assistants.

[27] Rozell 2014, p. 21.

[28] Goldrich 2011, p. 5.

[29] 713 F. Supp.2d 367 (S.D.N.Y. 2010).

The Court found that although injunctions are appropriate in disputes concerning works of art),[30] Robin's demand for relief had to be rejected because there was no writing expressing the agreement.

According to the New York Statute of Frauds (N.Y.U.C.C. § 2-201(1):

> A contract for the sale of goods for the price of $500 or more is not enforceable without a contemporaneous writing sufficient to indicate that a contract for sale has been made between the parties and signed by the parties against whom enforcement is sought.

5.5.2.1 Consigning Art

Most of the states in the USA, as well as the District of Columbia, have enacted legislation applicable to the consignment—common practice in the art world in USA—of art works to dealers by artists, their heirs, and their personal representatives.[31]

New York was the first state that enacted such a statute, in 1966, followed by California, in 1976, which used the New York's statute as a model. It must be stressed that these consignment laws that the states have passed, apply only to artists who consign their works to dealers; they do not apply to collectors who consign objects of their collections in the secondary (resale) market.[32]

Under the New York statute (Article 12 New York Arts and Cultural Affairs Law), art merchants have trust responsibilities and several specific obligations when they take art on consignment from an artist. The law was further strengthened in 2012 in response to the spectacular collapse of the Salander O'Reilly Gallery.

Since 1966, New York has required art merchants to treat artists as fiduciaries. Art delivered by an artist to an art merchant for exhibit or sale is deemed to be on consignment. The gallery is deemed to be the artist's agent.

A collector may, from necessity, boredom, or lack of interest on the part of the collector's heirs, decide to sell all or part of the collection. A dealer is contacted and a consignment agreement signed. The consignment agreement contains restrictions as to price, time, and category of buyer, and also, typically, provides that the collector can terminate the agreement for various reasons or no reason, and compel redelivery of the works not yet sold.[33]

The 2012 amendments to Section 12.01 of the NYACAL strengthen these protections and create criminal penalties for art merchants failing to meet these

---

[30] "Original works of art are within the small category of intrinsically unique goods for which specific performance remedy is appropriate", 713 F. Supp.2d 374 (S.D.N.Y. 2010), N.Y.U.C.C. § 2-716.

[31] Prowda 2013, p. 137.

[32] Prowda 2013, p. 137.

[33] Cahn 2011, p. 2.

requirements.[34] These amendments were long awaited. As it is pointed out, since November 6, 2012, when the amendments became effective, the consignee art merchant has "significant new duties and liabilities".[35]

5.5.2.2 Bankruptcy of the Gallery/Art Dealer

If the art dealer or the gallery files a bankruptcy proceeding, then both the artists and the collectors who had signed consignment agreements with the now bankrupt, might face a very difficult situation.

In the Salander Gallery bankruptcy case, art owners who had consigned works to the gallery found themselves confronted by a bankruptcy trustee who asserted that the bankrupt estate was now the owner of the art in question and the owner/consignor no longer had any rights to the works. This way, the owners/consignors appeared as just general unsecured creditors of the bankrupt gallery.

Some collectors charged Salander O'Reilly with selling consigned artwork and then failing to pay them their due proceeds.

In the case Jacobs v. Kraken Inv. Ltd. (In re Salander-O'Reilly Galleries, LLC), a consignor who had delivered a Boticelli painting to the Salander Gallery under a consignment agreement, became locked in a battle with the bankruptcy trustee over the priority of interests in the painting. The court held that the consignor did not necessarily have a right to the return of his work, but at the same time gave a consignor a possible leg up in its quest.[36]

The very difficult position of the Berry-Hill and Salander consignors in bankruptcy resulted from the curious treatment of consigned goods in bankruptcy. After its revision in 2001, most consignment transactions are governed by Article 9 of the Uniform Commercial Code. This means that if the consignor does not have a perfected security interest in an artwork, third party creditors may attach consigned artwork in a consignee's bankruptcy proceedings.

The policy rationale behind allowing third-party creditors to claim rights to consigned property was that the drafters of the Uniform Commercial Code did not want third parties to be harmed by "hidden liens" on a debtor's property.

Anyway, the amended New York statute explicitly states that the consigned artworks and their proceeds are considered property held in a statutory trust and they never become property of the art merchant or the art merchant's bankruptcy estate. It also provides that the trust property and the trust funds shall not be subordinated to any claim, lien, or security interest "of the consignee's creditors" (New York Arts and Cultural Affairs, § 2.01.1(a)(ii) and (iii)).[37]

[34] Wallace 2013, p. 9.

[35] Prowda 2013, p. 138.

[36] Cahn 2014, p. 7.

[37] Prowda 2013, p. 138.

References

Amineddoleh L (2014) Monuments men, hidden treasures, and the restitution of looted art. New York state bar assoc. Entertainment Arts Sports Law J 25:16–22

Cahn AR (2011) A funny thing happened on the way to the gallery: a bankruptcy fable (or not). Spencer's Art Law J 2(1):2–4

Cahn AR (2014) Yes, you can lose ownership of your art. Simply, consign to a gallery without giving public notice of your ownership, and under U.S. law, the gallery's trustee in bankruptcy will have a strong claim to your art. Spencer's Art Law J 5.1:7–9

Cruz Valdovinos JM (2013) Comercio Millonario del Estado Español en el siglo XX. Cuatro ejemplos y un botón de muestra. In: Socias I, Gkozgkou D (eds) Nuevas contribuciones en torno al mundo del coleccionismo de arte hispánico en los siglos XIX y XX, Ediciones Trea, Gijón (Asturias), pp 89–98

Detheridge A (2011) Quali diritti per l'arte contemporanea? In: Ajani G, Donati A (eds) I diritti dell′arte contemporanea. Umberto Allemandi & C, Torino, pp 25–36

Duarte A (2013) Da coleção ao museu: o colecionismo privado de arte moderna e contemporânea em Portugal. Revista Vox Musei arte e património 1:17–31

Fischer C (2012) Partner oder Kontrahenten? Eine rechtliche Untersuchung der Zusammenarbeit öffentlicher Museen und privater Kunstsammler. Nomos Verlagsgesellschaft, Baden-Baden

Fleck R (2013) Das Kunstsystem im 21. Jahrhundert. Museen, Künstler, Sammler, Galerien. Passagen Verlag, Wien

Goldrich AJ (2011) Is a right of first refusal an offer you can't refuse? If it's in writing, most probably. Spencer's Art Law J 2(1):5–9

González Sanz M, Montero de Espinosa Helly C (2011) Museos y mercado del arte. La adquisición de bienes culturales realizada por el Estado: una manera de recuperar, impulsar y difundir nuestro patrimonio. Arte y Sociedad. Revista de Investigación. http://www.eumed.net/rev/ays/0/gseh.html

Higonnet A (2010) A museums of one's own. Private collection, public gift. Periscope Publishing, Pittsburgh

Jardine L (2013) A point of view: the art of collecting, BBC News magazine. http://www.bbc.com/news/magazine-2160204?print=true

Kadelbach S (1997) Kommunaler Kulturbetrieb, Freiheit der Kunst und Privatrechtsform. Neue Juristische Wochenschrift 50:1114–1119

Lundén S (2005) TV review: NRK (Norway), Skriftsamleren [The Manuscript Collector]. Cult Without Context 16:3–11

Prowda JB (2013) Visual arts and the law. A handbook for professionals. Lund Humphries in Association with Sotheby's Institute of Art, Farnham

Rozell M (2014) The art collector's handbook. A guide to collection management and care. Lund Humphries in Association with Sotheby's Institute of Art, Farnham

Sax JL (1999) Playing darts with a Rembrandt. Public and private rights in cultural treasures. The University of Michigan Press, Ann Arbor

Von Zezschwitz F (1983) Rechtsstaatliche und prozessuale Probleme des Verwaltungsprivatrechts. Neue Juristische Wochenschrift 1873–1882

Wallace J (2013) Consigning art under New York's amended arts and cultural affairs law: lessons for artists, their estates, and collectors. Spencer's Art Law J 4(2):8–11

Chapter 6
Governance of Museums

6.1 General Comments

Very few comparative law texts have been written on the subject of the museums' governance.[1] On the contrary, there have been published many commentaries, articles, books, on the economic aspects of museums' governance, approaching the museum as enterprise, as organization of human and financial resources, as a considerable factor for the production of a State's richness.[2]

A very important reason for this scarcity of legal texts is, as it is pointed out, that at about 20 years ago a new sort of research started, on new juridical instruments that could be used for the governance of museums. The fact that many countries all these years have been forced to restrain the State budget, led to new forms of governance, the juridical regulation of which is still a work in progress.

There are many differences between the States, concerning the existence (or not) of specific legislation that defines the concept of "museum" and sets the prerequisites that should be met for its acceptance.[3]

As it is brilliantly presented, the differences between the national laws are very much depended on many and diverse factors, among which the traditions, the culture, the history of each State are included.

In some countries, things are absolutely clear: National museums are exclusively funded by the State. This is the case, for example, of South Korea, where the law does not permit that the national museums be supported by private companies.[4] In other countries, the private sector is very powerful. There are also cases in between: growing participation of the private sector in the museums' governance, in countries where in the past it was not permitted, but also heated discussions about whether this could or should happen.

---

1 Crismani 2013.
2 Cerrina Feroni 2010, p. 81.
3 Cerrina Feroni 2010, p. 83.
4 Park 2014.

E. Moustaira, *Art Collections, Private and Public: A Comparative Legal Study*, SpringerBriefs in Law, DOI 10.1007/978-3-319-15802-0_6

There are voices speaking in favor of a so called "democratization" of the museum universe. An ambivalent term probably, as far as museums are concerned, it mostly shows the tendency of some countries—USA, for example—museums to become "spectacular" didactic institutions.

The supporters of such a development insist that accessibility is the key word, accessibility not only for the disabled persons but mostly an intellectual accessibility, as they argue. According to this view, what the U.S. museums try to do is to make as much as more pleasurable the experience of learning. In this line, the objects of the museums' collections are not the aim but the means to their mission which is the public service, independently of whether they are public museums or non-profit museums governed by private persons.[5]

The Metropolitan Museum of Art, of New York, is used as an example for the above arguments. This museum had, since its foundation in 1870, developed editorial and *merchandising* activity. Nowadays, the Metropolitan Museum has a vast program of these activities. As it is argued, and it can hardly be doubted, the success of the commercial activities of the museum depends on the constant effort to maintain a high quality in whatever it does.

Prudently, to the question whether it would be possible to replicate the Metropolitan Museum in some other country (in this case, in Italy), the answer that is offered is a nuanced no. It is added thought, that pertinent elements of such an activity could be added to this other country's legal system.[6]

6.2 China

In some countries, things are changing these last years and sometimes they are changing fast. One such example is China. Generally speaking, the country's legal regime for cultural property "with Chinese characteristics" is an important part of the Chinese legal system.[7]

As it is stated, during the last decades, many facts have very much influenced the evolution of the museum's sector. New museums' governance problems emerged, due to processes of modernization of the relevant professional activities.

The economic growth of the country had enormous repercussions on the cultural patrimony: the construction of big infrastructures and the transformation of the urban context on the one hand led to the discovery—and often the destruction—of new archaeological finds and on the other hand menace the existent cultural monuments.[8]

[5] Berger 2010, p. 196.

[6] Berger 2010, p. 200.

[7] Huo 2014, p. 154.

[8] Zan and Bonini Baraldi 2014.

Most museums in China are public or indirectly financed and controlled by the state.[9] They are organized in three levels: national, provincial and local. The [public] institutions that deal with the management of museums are structured over four levels: governmental, provincial, prefectural and county.

The main authority is the State Administration of Cultural Heritage, which is based in Beijing. It falls under the Ministry of Culture and supervises all the lower levels of management. Among other responsibilities, it formulates museum policies and regulations, supervises their implementation, coordinates professionals' activities, selects the sites to be protected, supervises archeological excavations and consults on the creation of new museums.[10]

It seems that up to a certain point, this exclusivity of the public sector as far as museums are concerned, has started to change. Thus, the Guanfu Museum of Classic Arts, the first privately-owned museum of China, an officially approved and registered corporate body, opened its doors in 1997.

6.3 Italy

In Italy there have been made, since many years, researches about the role of museums. It is pointed out that when museums for the first time proposed themselves as museums for all people, the problems of governance were revealed, because of various reasons, among which are the following: the difficult compatibility between art objects and mass visits, the lack of resources, the difficulties of conservation and protection, the fact that some of them in the beginning had been structured as private buildings not to be open to an indiscriminate public.[11]

Article 150 para 4 of the Law Decree 112/1998 transferred the governance of the State museums to the Regions and to local entities. By doing so, it strengthened and stabilized the principle of autonomous exercise of museums' activities. Law Decree 368/1998 (Article 8 para 4) and Presidential Decree 441/2000 established le Soprintendenze speciali for the museums of Rome, Florence, Venice and Naples.[12]

This autonomy does not exclude directory acts by the responsible Ministry or the public entity to which museums refer. As it is pointed out, this autonomy is non-existent as far as organization, financing and accounting are concerned.[13] There are rarely documents testifying their financing, they do not have their own personnel (people working at the museums usually fall under the Ministry, or the region, the

---

[9] Varutti 2014, p. 43.

[10] Varutti 2014, p. 44.

[11] Denuzzo 2013a.

[12] Denuzzo 2013b.

[13] Crismani 2013.

province, the commune, or other entity), they do not always have scientific committees, nor have their own patrimonial documents or regulations.[14]

In 2001, a ministerial decree defined the museum standards that theoretically would facilitate a formal definition of the museums' juridical status, since they would dispose of a statute or a regulation or some other written document. It seems though that the museums rarely have such documents.[15]

According to a well-based opinion, the reason for which this transfer of governance of museums took place was the lack of a real tradition of national unity. The 150 and more years of political unity have not been enough to create a concept of "Italian" cultural property.[16] On the contrary, the local identity of Italians has been and still is much stronger than their "national" one. This fact has several consequences, one of which would be the unwillingness to have a central, national, care and governance of the cultural institutions, among which one should count the museums.[17]

This local identity of the Italians, which is often stronger than their relatively recent national identity, has historic and cultural roots founded in the political mosaic of the country. Most of all, the reason would be the rich cultural property of the states which formed this mosaic, such as: il Regno dei due Sicilie, il Grande Ducato deToscana, i Ducati de Parma e Modena, la Reppublica di Genova. As it is very clearly pointed out, following the War of Independence of the 19th century, the Italian nation inherited those properties. The fact exactly that it has inherited and not created the so called Italian cultural property has made it impossible to amalgamate the various local identities and create a "profound national identity".[18]

Thus, it is not really a surprise the fact that, willing to privatize as much as possible of the governance of the public cultural patrimony, the definition of the museum in the Codice dei Beni Culturali does not contain the "non-profit" character of it. This is contrary to what happens in the majority of the States of free market regime, where the museums are almost unexceptionally considered as non-profit organizations.[19] This latter is due to the fact that in most States it has been realized that the governance of the cultural institutions is not profitable in terms of direct earnings and that the social value of cultural identity is a good that should be protected from the interference of the commercialization.[20]

---

[14] Forte 2010.

[15] Sciullo 2001; Barbati 2008.

[16] But see Settis 2005, p. 73: "la funzione civile del patrimonio artistico si e sempre esercitata in Italia mediante un meccanismo duplice, il controllo pubblico e l'identita civica, entrambe da intendersi in senso territoriale e diffuso, una sorta di eredita che si trasmette da una generazione all'altra per comunanza di orizzonti cuturali non meno che per un assetto normativo che la perpetua e la favorisce".

[17] Pinna 2009–2010, p. 70.

[18] Pinna 2009–2010, p. 70.

[19] In USA, Museum and Library Services Act states that the museum is "a public or private non-profit agency or institution". The same is provided in other countries too, for example Ireland, Australia, Israel, etc.

[20] Pinna 2005, p. 55.

The argument is put forth that one of the biggest difficulties in the Italian system of museums is the complexity and diversity of their governance, especially of the museums of contemporary art. The history museums have a structured organization and they are mostly governed by the sovrintendenze.

On the contrary, the museums of contemporary art are communal, regional, provincial, and, recently, one state museum was established. As far as their juridical structure is concerned, these museums are foundations, associations, etc.

This diversity, according to the above arguments, is an obstacle to a systematization of the Italian museums system.[21]

Other voices are more lenient and do not consider this sort of pluralism as something negative. On the contrary, they consider the plurality of contents, of subjects, of forms of culture, as an expression of the democracy and pluralism of the Italian legal order.[22]

This pluralism invites for cooperation between public and private,[23] they say. And the reasons and instruments of this cooperation owe their existence to the deepest characteristics of the Italian system of cultural objects. The so called complexity, they say, in reality is the expression of the constitutional principles of social pluralism (Articles 2 and 18 Italian Constitution), of institutional pluralism (Articles 5 and 114 ff Italian Constitution) and of guarantees of freedom of culture and research (Article 33 ff Italian Constitution), and more generally, it is the manifestation of thought (Article 21 Italian Constitution) and of economic initiative (Article 41 Italian Constitution).

Furthermore, the Italian Constitution foresees cases of straight cooperation between the state and the regions (Article 118, comma 3, Italian Constitution), concerning the cultural objects, and at the same time, the possibility that a certain state law, result of an agreement between the State and an interested Region, attributes forms of autonomy to the Regions that submitted such a request (Article 116, comma 3, Italian Constitution).[24]

6.3.1 Musei Ecclesiastici

The subject of the ecclesiastical museums has occupied only a small, reduced space[25] of the rich production of juridical texts on cultural objects of religious interest, it is pointed out. The reasons for this are, on the one hand the fact that there are very few legal norms on this subject, on the other hand the opinion of many jurists, at least

[21] Eccher 2011, p. 80.
[22] Cammelli 2011, p. 175.
[23] Cammelli 2007.
[24] Cammelli 2011, p. 194.
[25] Renna 2005.

in the past, that the museums—and the ecclesiastical ones even more—cannot be considered as cultural objects per se.[26]

This mentality has changed, since nowadays it is a common belief that museums are themselves cultural objects.

And as what must be considered the ecclesiastical museums, public or private? In Italy, they answer this question as follows: According to the Article 101 of the Codice Urbani, the museum is included in the ambit of the "Institutes and places of culture" (*Istituti e luoghi di cultura*) and it is identified as "a permanent structure that acquires, conserves, puts in order and exposes cultural objects with the aim of education and study" (*una struttura permanente che acquisisce, conserva, ordina ed espone beni culturali per finalità di educazione e di studio*).

This definition, which approaches the one that ICOM has included in its Statute, follows the tendencies of the modern museology, focusing in the organizational profile of the museum, that is, in its activities, and abandoning the traditional approach that for a long time considered the museum as the total of its objects (universitas rerum).[27]

The same Article 101 of the Codice Urbani, nos 3 and 4, determines the juridical regime of the museums, by saying that when they belong to a public subject, "they are destined to the public fruition and perform a public service" (*sono destinati alla pubblica fruizione ed espletano un servizio pubblico*), while when they belong to private subjects and at the same time are open to the public, "perform a private service of social utility" (*espletano un servizio privato di utilitàsociale*).

According to the above definitions, it is said, it would seem correct to conclude that the ecclesiastical museums are private ones and that if they are open to the public,[28] they perform a "private service of social utility".[29]

As far as the canonic regulations are concerned, let us mention the fundamental Norme (della Conferenza Episcopale Italiana) of 1974, adopted by CEI, the point 10 of which was wholly dedicated to the museums and the exposition's rooms. After having reminded that "the art objects must remain, possibly, in the places of worship in order to conserve for the churches, the orators, the monasteries and convents the significant aspect of the original physiognomy of the places destined to worship", it was recommended that where such conservation at the original places was no more possible, "diocesan or interdiocesan museums" or proper exposition's rooms should be instituted.

The 1974 Norms were not excluding that, in absence of ecclesiastical museums or in case these could not guarantee adequate conditions for the conservation, valorization and security, the art objects could be deposited, by contract, temporarily in the State museums or in the museums of other public entities.[30]

---

26 Chizzoniti and Margiotta Broglio 2010, p. 142.

27 Severini 2003.

28 It is not obligatory. This open access is regulated by Article 104 of the Codice Urbani.

29 Denuzzo 2013a.

30 Chizzoniti and Margiotta Broglio 2010, p. 146.

In 1992, CEI reviewed the 1974 Norms in a document with the title "I beni culturali della Chiesa. Orientamenti".[31] It reconfirms the central role of the diocesan museum, "natural point of reference for the analogous ecclesiastical institutions" (*naturale punto di riferimento per le analogue istituzioni ecclesiastiche*).

In 2001, the Pontificia Commissione per i beni culturali has sent to the bishops a circular Letter "The pastoral function of the museums" (*La funzione pastorale dei musei*), in which, among other things, underlines the role that the museums must play for the care, the valorization and the promotion of the ecclesiastical cultural objects. In this circular letter, the museum is defined as "the place that documents the evolution of the cultural and religious life" (*il luogo che documenta l'evolversi della vita culturale e religiosa*).

6.4 Germany

In this country, the argument of "museum's enterprise" is very strong. Article 33 para 6 of the German Constitution (*Grundgesetz*): part of the doctrine believes that freedom of both art and science provide the frame for an "institutional guarantee" of the museums and of those who work in and for them.

Contrary to what happens in Italy and in other countries, in Germany there is no federal constitutional recognition of the protection of cultural objects. It is the Länder which have the legislative power concerning the governance, the valorization, the conservation of those cultural objects. The Constitutions of the Länder do contain specific provisions concerning the promotion and the care of cultural objects/heritage. For example, Article 3 of the Bayern Constitution stresses the fact that the Land is a social State and a State of Law, but it is also a "Kulturstaat". This article and others too specify the duties of the Land and of the Gemeindeverbände concerning details of promotion and care of cultural life.

The Constitutions of almost all the other Länder contain analogous provisions. For example, Constitution of Berlin, Article 20, Constitution of Mecklenburg-Vorpommern, Article 16, Constitution of Sachsen, Article 11, Constitution of Sachsen-Anhalt, Article 36.[32]

As it is mentioned, the cardinal principle of the German Federal Constitution is the neutrality of the State as far as culture is concerned, in order to guarantee a cultural development free of State influence. In Germany, there is no juridical definition whatever of the "museum" and there are no specific federal laws about museums. General laws of public law are applied as well as the provisions of Civil Code, Versicherungsvetragsgesetze, etc.

---

[31] Feliciani 1998, points out that even though these "Orientations" have no legislative force, they are not deprived from authority. According to the general principles concerning the decisions of the conferences, the bishops (*vescovi*) may avoid to conform to such orientations only in serious cases of conscience, something that would seem absolutely improbable in this case.

[32] Cerrina Feroni 2010, p. 105, n. 59.

On the contrary, there are federal laws which concern single museums or groups of museums and which have as their aim/object the establishment and the organization of Foundations (*Stiftungen*) which will have the responsibility for those museums' governance.

Comparing the Italian and the German system, according to one opinion the second is simpler. There are private associations—Kunstvereine—where galleries, collectors, even artists in some cases, are included, "intermediate" entities, like Kunsthalle, which belong to the state but they have no permanent collections, and Kunstmuseen, which do have permanent collections.[33]

Two decades ago, Germany started researching for new forms of museums' governance. This research reached its peak at the beginning of the new millennium, when a crisis hit the German economy and the public entities had to face a growing deficit which was demanding cuts. Culture was one of the first public sections which suffered the respective repercussions. The various problems that were created, contributed to the lack of attraction of the public museums for those persons of the private section who would think about financing them.

All these problems revealed the need to find new juridical forms of governance for the public museums, in order for them to become more autonomous as far as financing and organization are concerned. Various forms were established, with various grades of autonomy.

6.4.1 Stiftungen Des Öffentlichen Rechts

It is one of the more preferred juridical forms since the second half of the '90s, instituted by law of the Länder. There is no unitary discipline of these foundations; each Land has different provisions for them in their respective Stiftungsgesetze. Nevertheless, there can be traced some common characteristics.

According to the Bundesverfassungsgericht, they have to pursue aims of public utility and must be in "straight organizational correlation" with a public organ. The Stiftungsgesetze of the Länder provide that they have to be instituted by a public authority and have a juridical personality of their own. In case of the Museumsstiftungen of public law, they may be instituted by the Bund or by a Land, in order to manage one or more museums. Most of the times they become proprietary of the museum's objects, but there are cases in which they only acquire the governance of the museum which remains property of the Land. In some cases, the Stiftung has the duty to institute herself a museum not yet existing.

The aims of all those foundations, according to the Museumsstiftungsgesetze, are the acquisition, conservation, exposition of cultural objects, as well as the research and communication. They have their own directive organs: a Presidency (*Vorstand*), that is the responsible for the governance of the foundation and

[33] Eccher 2011, p. 80.

therefore of the museum, a Council (*Stiftungsrat*) and a scientific Committee (*Beirat*)—the last one is not always foreseen.[34]

The functions of the different organs of the foundations vary enough. There are also differences among them as far as their autonomy from the public authority is concerned. Nevertheless, the State is always surveying (*Staatsaufsicht*) whether the operation of the foundation is in conformity with the State's legal order.

A part of the financing of the foundations is covered by the national budget, but there is always the possibility to also receive private financing for which tax deductions are foreseen, given the fact that the foundations pursue aims of public utility.

A very interesting and complex example of the German museum system is the Stiftung "Preussischer Kulturbesitz" (foundation of public law), which falls directly under the Federation (*Bund*).[35] It was established by a federal law of 25.7.1957 (Gesetz zur Errichtung einer Stiftung "Preussischer Kulturbesitz" und zur Übertragung von Vermögenswerten des ehemaligen Landes Preussen auf die Stiftung). It was last amended on 29.10.2001.[36]

It is the biggest existing German cultural institution, responsible for the governance of the most important German museums (a group of 16 museums in Berlin) but also of other relevant institutions, as for example the State Library of Berlin (*Staastbibliothek zu Berlin*) and the Secret Archive of the Prussian patrimony (*Geheimes Staatsarchiv*).

6.5 Spain

Articles 148.1.15 and 149.1.28 of the Spanish Constitution distribute the competences upon Archives, Libraries and Museums between the State and the Autonomous Communities (*Comunidades Autónomas*).

One can classify the museums in three big categories: (1) Museums owned by the State and managed by it, either through the Ministry of Culture or through some other entity created specifically for that; (2) Museums owned by the State and managed by the Comunidades Autónomas; and (3) Museums owned by the Comunidades Autónomas or local communities or belonging to private persons.

The museums of the second category are of great importance because of their big quantity and because of their respective revenues. Until today the issue whether their ownership could be transferred to the Comunidades Autónomas has not been resolved.[37]

---

34 Cerrina Feroni 2010, pp. 106–108.

35 Carnevale 2010, p. 235.

36 The text of the law may be found in: http://www.hv.spk-berlin.de/deutsch/wir_ueber_uns/download/Stiftungsgesetz2001.pdf.

37 Barrero Rodríguez 2009, p. 37.

There are eight Comunidades Autónomas that have adopted a law specifically for museums.[38] There are also specific rules on museums in the legislation of other Comunidades Autónomas that regulates the historical patrimony. This is the case of the Comunidades Autónomas: Canarias, Extremadura, Galicia and País Vasco.[39]

The State Rules on Museums are: the Law on Spanish Historical Patrimony (*La Ley del Patrimonio Histórico Español*), of 1985, and the Regulation on the Spanish System of Museums (*el Reglamento del Sistema Español de Museos*), approved by the Royal Decree of 1987.

This State legislation is only applied on the museums owned by the State and on those that, although they are owned by the State, "enter" the Spanish system of museums by a signed agreement.[40]

The Spanish legislation on museums and on the cultural patrimony does not contain anything about the juridical structure of the museums. However, it does take into account the diversity of the functions that nowadays museums have and that in the past were only mentioned in individual studies or in "soft law", such as declarations and deontological norms.[41]

6.5.1 Museo Del Prado: A New Juridical Regime

Museo del Prado represents one of the best answers to the questions posed on the subject of the "new museum", the museum of our era, it is declared.[42]

At first (1785) it was dedicated to the Natural Sciences, some years afterwards it hosted the Spanish Royal Collection of paintings and sculptures and at last, in 1819 it opened its doors to the public.

During the recent decades, we assist at various efforts to redefine the aims of the museums and of the cultural politics in general. In the frame of all these "movements", the Spanish legislator invented a peculiar regime specifically for the Museo del Prado.

Following long parliamentary discussions, a law (*Ley* no. 46/25.11.2003) and a Law Decree (*Real Decreto*, 12.3.2004), approving the new statute of the museum, were promulgated.

The "new social orientation" was taken into account, so that the big museum would be the seat of cultural evolution, of study, of construction of the national identity of the whole community.[43]

By the Law 46/2003 a new kind of public entity has been created, a "public organism of special character". It is a hybrid juridical regime: a juridical regime of

[38] About the museums in Andalucia, see Caruz Arcos 2009, p. 41.

[39] Stampa 2007, p. 20.

[40] Stampa 2007, p. 20.

[41] Stampa 2009, p. 52.

[42] Brunori 2010, p. 223.

[43] Brunori 2010, p. 227.

public law with the possibility to act according the rules of private law, respecting though the "Ley General Presupuestaria", no. 47/2003, which regulates the regime of State domain, public and private.

The museum, the juridical nature of which remains public ("El Museo Nacional del Prado es un organismo público", Article 1, Law 46/2003), has a specific financing regime, permanently controlled by the Intervención General de la Administración General del Estado.

Among the specific characteristics of this "new regime" are the following: The contractual activity of the museum has to respect the Law on Contracts of Public Administration, with the possibility, concerning specifically the "commercial activities" of the museum, to operate according the principles of private law, respecting though the principles of publicity and pluralism.

The museum is the proprietor of its own patrimony, distinct from that of the State. The acquisition of immovable property is subordinated to the permission of the Ministry of Finance. In general, a large liberty is conferred to the museum as far as the management of products and the income of its own capital are concerned. It is also provided that it is possible to receive donations or heritage or legs by private persons.[44]

It is argued that this combination of public and private characteristics of the museum does not create disequilibrium. It is even suggested that this "new museum's" characteristics—novelty, hybridization, specialty—are the key words that should be taken into account in order to think about the big museums of the future.[45]

6.6 France

In France, the concept of "museum" is expressly defined in the Code du patrimoine and the law 2002-5 of 2002 (that since 2004 has become part of the Code du patrimoine, L441) has regulated in a unitary way the "Musées de France".

The qualification of "Musée de France" may be attributed to the collections that belong to the State, to public entities, and also to non-profit legal entities of private law. In order to acquire this qualification, the interested museum has to file an application and an administrative proceeding has to take place, in which the Haut Conseil des Musées de France participates too. This organ has been instituted by the above law (Article 3) and has a consultative competence. It is constituted by members of the Assemblée Nationale, representatives of the central government and of the local administration, professionals of the museums and experts.

An absolutely fundamental prerequisite for the above denomination is that the conservation and the exhibition of the museum's collections are important for

[44] Cerrina Feroni 2010, pp. 134–135.

[45] Brunori 2010, p. 232.

the "general interest" (*l'intérêt general*).[46] The moment a museum ceases being of that interest, the qualification of "Musée de France" may be revoked via a decision of the administrative authority, having first consulted the Haut Conseil des Musées de France (Article 4).

The aims of the Musées de France are: to conserve, restore, study and enrich their own collections, make these collections accessible to the biggest possible number of persons, conceive and put in praxis educational activities that will ensure for all people access to culture, contribute to the progress of knowledge and of research as well as of their diffusion (Article 2).[47]

6.7 Canada—USA

Both in Canada and in the United States, most museums are incorporated as non-profit entities under provincial or state statute law. In some cases, particular institutions are incorporated by individual statutes.[48] Examples of the latter are the National Gallery of Canada, which was established by the federal 1990 Museums Act[49] and the Smithsonian Institution, which was established by a 1846 Act of Congress.[50]

If a museum is not incorporated, it operates as a charitable trust or in some other form of unincorporated association. Different statutory and common law rules apply to them.

In both countries, institutions established as museums are deemed in law to hold their property for a charitable purpose for the benefit of the public.[51] It is the common law that determines whether a museum is a charity.

The traditional responsibility to enforce charitable trusts or gifts rests, in both Canada and the United States, with the attorney general of the jurisdiction where the charity is located. That means that in cases involving charities, the only person who has standing to sue is the attorney-general. The basic reason for that is that a charitable gift benefits the public and not the individuals.

There have been attempts in United States to expand standing to sue to other persons too, in cases involving charities, on the ground that more persons—charity constituencies—become involved in how museums, as charities, are managed.

---

46 On this, see Cornu and Mallet-Poujol 2006, p. 25.

47 Cerrina Feroni 2010, pp. 91–92.

48 Paterson 2013.

49 S.C. 1990, c.3.

50 20 U.S.C. §§ 41–80 (2000).

51 According to U.S. Restatement (Second) of the Law of Trusts, § 368: "A purpose is charitable if its accomplishment is of such social interest to the community as to justify permitting the property to be devoted to the purpose in perpetuity".

Thus, the attorney-general may permit a person to sue in his or her stead, by granting him/her relator status.[52]

In Canada there are fewer private-funded museums than in USA. Many institutions governed by the Canadian government have chosen the corporate form of legal association. The federal 1990 Museums Act establishes several national museums as Crown (government) corporations. They—as all the other Canadian museums—are also charitable institutions. There is a fiduciary relationship between the trustees and directors of museums and the museums themselves. In case there are claims about them breaching their fiduciary duty—for example, while undertaking commercial activities aimed at increasing the economic efficiency of the museum, it will be the federal or provincial attorneys general the ones who will have standing to bring such claims before the courts.[53]

More specifically, the following may be stated about the governance of museums in these two countries:

6.7.1 Canada

In Canada, the big development of the museums started at the time of the celebrations for the centenary of the Confederation, in 1967. The federal government and the governments of the provinces established "a net of modern museums sharing the same philosophy" as the museums of USA.[54]

In Canada, two models of governance are observed. In the common law provinces, the museums' functions resemble a lot to that of the U.S. museums. In the francophone province, things are different. Except of five national museums, the net of museums in Quebec comprises non-profit organisms that function as private institutions that depend on the administration's councils. The three levels of the country's government—cities, provincial government and federal government—assume more than 46 % of the financing of the museum institutions.

In Quebec, the private voluntaries are also important for the funding of museums, but less than what is happening in the rest of the country and in USA. Evidently, Quebec proposes an intermediate model between the one in Northern America and the ones in the European countries.[55] Furthermore, it is stated that the government of Quebec is by far the Canadian province that spends the most in culture.[56]

---

52 Paterson 2013.

53 Paterson 2007, p. 421.

54 Bergeron and Frey 2013, p. 19.

55 About Quebec as a mixed jurisdiction, see Moustaira 1995, pp. 298–299.

56 Bergeron 2009–2010, p. 62.

6.7.2 USA

In USA, before the 1960s, there was not much direct support for the arts which were mostly relying on favorable treatment under the property and income taxes.[57] This reliance on tax subsidies may be considered as an American characteristic according to which charitable donations support many services that in other countries are provided by the government.

The turning point in the U.S. federal policy towards the arts was in 1965, when the National Foundation on the Arts and Humanities was set up, after several years of heated debate in Congress. Two separate funding agencies were instituted, the National Endowment for the Arts and the National Endowment for the Humanities, both authorized to make grants to individuals and institutions.[58]

Grants were to be made only for specific projects and of course private funds would be absolutely necessary. In order to be clear that undue control would be not permitted, it was stated in the bill: "No department, agency, officer, or employee of the United States shall exercise any direction, supervision, or control over the policy determination, personnel, or curriculum or the administration or operation of any school or other non-Federal agency, institution, organization, or association".

As it is stated, the direct federal funding for the arts in the United States has been always much smaller than government support in countries of Western Europe. For example, at about the beginning of the 1980s, it was suggested that the per capita federal spending on cultural agencies was no more than one-third of the comparable amount in Italy or one-fifth of the comparable amount in France and Sweden.[59]

The National Gallery of Art and the other federal museums in Washington, D.C. are the museums to which most of the federal funding is directed. They are geographically concentrated in the national capital and they are open to the public free of charge.[60]

It is a fact that, although there are some excellent art museums in small cities, nevertheless there is a disproportionate concentration of large and well-funded museums in the great metropolitan areas of the United States. It is estimated that "museum funding flows to the metropolitan areas roughly in proportion to the attendance figures".[61]

It is estimated that the federal government's indirect subsidies for art museums are at least as large as its direct funding.

[57] Clotfelter 1991, p. 238.

[58] Clotfelter 1991, p. 239.

[59] Clotfelter 1991, p. 245 and n. 24.

[60] Offering the public free access to their exhibitions is a central purpose for many museums, according to Rosett 1991, p. 144.

[61] Rosett 1991, pp. 132, 134.

6.8 United Kingdom

In United Kingdom, most museums are all-purpose (with scientific, technological, and art collections) and only a few of them focus only on fine and decorative art.[62]

Government support was the major source for the many national and local museums—it still is a major source. At the beginning it was only reluctantly that it assumed the task of financing museums and art galleries.

During the 19th century private collections were growing and opened to the public on request. The National Gallery of British Art (renamed, later, Tate Gallery) opened in 1897. It was by the late 1920s that state funding was completely established.[63]

In 1988, the Museums & Galleries Commission[64] adopted the Registration Scheme for Museums and Galleries, containing the prerequisites and the characteristics—the minimum standards—that a museum should have in order to be able to register as such—as museum.[65]

The aims of this were and are to construct a network of the British museums, in order that: (a) these would share common minimum standards as far as their quality and the accessibility to the public is concerned, maintaining at the same time their governing autonomy; (b) the fide that the collectivity has to museum institutions would be accrued, so that the museums may be considered, perceived as keepers of goods of public interest; (c) an ethical base common to all the museums would be created, by having common codes of ethics and by following common politics.[66]

This Registration Scheme for Museums and Galleries was first revised in 1995 and then in 2004, when it was renamed Accreditation Scheme for Museums. The last revision was made by the Museums, Libraries and Archives Council, a Non-Departmental Public Body which was established in 2000, falls under the Museums and Galleries Commission and is responsible for the museums, the libraries and the archives.

---

[62] Clarke 1991, p. 271.

[63] Clarke 1991, p. 274.

[64] This Commission was established in 1931, as an organ of the British Government, and in its responsibilities are included the following: representing the museums and galleries' interests, being a council to the museums, as well as promoting and diffusing the museum culture.

[65] The need had been felt to organize a unitary scheme, a unitary discipline for all English museums. This was a sort of transplant of the strategy that the *Association of American Museums* had adopted in USA, see Cerrina Feroni 2010, p. 88.

[66] Cerrina Feroni 2010, p. 89.

6.9 Archives

In some countries a new discipline has been developed, that of the organization of archives and of their protection as cultural objects. One of these countries is France, co-founder of the International Council of Archives (*Conseil international des archives*), responsible for the organization of the First International Congress on Archives and having set since the 50s' an international educational net of exchanges on the theory and praxis of organizing archives.[67]

The close relationship between France and Quebec, the mixed jurisdiction of Canada, led naturally to the development of this discipline there too. Quebec and, in general, Canada is one of the 20 first importers of French art objects among 154 countries—Quebec imports the 60 % of them.[68]

It is since the 19th century that a cultural association had taken the initiative to enlarge the already existing collection of archives concerning Canada and the Canadians—term that, at that time (19th century), was referring to the native habitants or of French descent. This cultural association was the Quebec Literary and Historical Society, which in 1826 published the "Histoire du Canada depuis sa découverte jusqu'à l'année 1791".

The same need of finding their traces had already been felt by the historians of USA since the beginning of the 19th century. Therefore, in 1841, the Legislature of the State of New York had charged John Romeyn Brodhead with a 3 years mission in Holland, England and France. He had returned from these countries with 6,000 pages of documents' copies, which were published.[69]

During the last years, the archivist cooperation between Canada and France has been even more intensified, something that has not really happened between Canada and England. In 2004, when the commemorations for the 400th anniversary of the French presence in Canada started, culminating in 2008, with the 400th anniversary of the Quebec's foundation, the portal Archives Canada—France was created.

As it is pointed out, the clustering of documents relating to the European colonization of North America has been accomplished thanks to: the work of jurists and historians, the positive action of Canada and of the Quebec's government as well as the collaboration of French and English archives' departments.[70]

In Mexico, there is a tradition of protection of the documents that are considered valuable for the society. This tradition goes back to the time before the arrival of Europeans in America. According to reliable sources, the native peoples of the territory that today is Mexico, had libraries for codices.[71]

---

[67] Grailles-Marcilloux 2013, p. 47.

[68] Marcilloux 2013, p. 73.

[69] Litalien 2013, p. 35.

[70] Litalien 2013, pp. 43–44.

[71] Armendáriz Sánchez 2009, p. 83.

On 23.1.2012 the Diario Oficial de la Federación promulgated the Federal Law of Archives (*Ley Federal de Archivos*) which regulates the General Archive of the Nation (*Archivo General de la Nación*). According to the Article 41 of this new law, the General Archive of the Nation is a decentralized organ of the Federal Public Administration.[72]

This law is considered as reflecting progress in various points: One of them is that it creates juridical definitions of the documental patrimony and especially of the historical archive. The Mexican juridical system has two legal concepts of the historical archive.

The first is contained in the Federal Law on archaeological, artistic and historical monuments and zones (*Ley federal sobre monumentos y zonas arqueológicos, artísticos e históricos*), of 1972. According to that law, are included in the historical archive "the documents and files that belong or have belonged to the offices and archives of the Federation, the states or the municipalities and the curial houses. Also the original handwritten documents related to the history of Mexico and the books, leaflets and other printed in Mexico or abroad, during the 16th–19th centuries, which because of their rarity and importance for the Mexican history, deserve to be conserved in the country".[73]

The second concept, contained in the Ley Federal de Archivos, extends the ambit of protection to the documents the origin of which is more recent, but which are important for the "collective memory of Mexico" (*la memoria colectiva de México*) and fundamentals "for the knowledge of the national history" (*para el conocimiento de la historia nacional*).

Very few things have been written on the subject of ecclesiastical archives.[74] For example, in Spain, it is only after the promulgation of the Law of 1985 (Ley de Patrimonio Histórico Español) that a few articles and books were written on this subject.[75]

---

[72] Berrueco García 2014, pp. 62–63.

[73] "los documentos y expedientes que pertenezcan o hayan pertenecido a las oficinas y archivos de la Federación, de los estados o de los municipios relacionados con la historia de México y los libros, folletos y otros impresos en México o en el extranjero, durante los siglos XVI al XIX que por su rareza e importancia para la historia mexicana, merezcan ser conservados en el país".

[74] As it is very well said, documents are conserved in archives and the archives are the custodians of memory. The ecclesiastical archives are considered as constituting privileged fountains of knowledge of the social, political, economic history.

[75] Cano Ruiz 2012, p. 177. She mentions one very detailed study/article that had been written before the 1985 legislation—in 1972.

6.10 Concluding Comments

The most recent studies on the governance of museums in various countries, under various national laws, have shown that all the new laws which had as their aim to modernize the museums' system have not led to a unitary model of museum.[76]

This fact rather means that it is not possible to have a uniform approach to the museums' discipline; on the contrary, it only seems possible to construct general schemes in the frame of which every single museum could have its own organization settled.

References

Armendáriz Sánchez S (2009) Los códices y la biblioteca prehispánica y su influencia en las bibilotecas conventuales en México. Biblioteca Universitaria 12:83–103

Barbati C (2008) Gli standard nazionali di qualita per le professioni museali; le prospettive possibili. Aedon 2008 no 1. http://www.aedon.mulino.it/archivio/2008/1/barbati.htm

Barrero Rodríguez C (2009) Algunas notas sobre el régimen jurídico de los museos de titularidad estatal y gestión autonómica en la Comunidad Autónoma de Andalucía. Revista de los museos de Andalucía 11:36–40

Berger D (2010) Il Metropolitan Museum of Art di New York. Il merchandising come mezzo di promozione. In: Morbidelli G, Cerrina Feroni G (a cura di) I musei. Discipline, gestioni, prospettive. G. Giappichelli Editore, Torino, pp 195–200

Bergeron Y (2009–2010) Los museos y la crisis. Tendencias en los museos norteamericanos. Revista Museos 5–6:58–67

Bergeron Y, Frey V (2013) Deixis: du théâtre des objets au théâtre de l'histoire. In: Bergeron Y, Frey V (dir) Archives et musées. Le théâtre du patrimoine (France–Canada). Editions du Comité des travaux historiques et scientifiques, pp 13–29

Berrueco García A (2014) Antecedentes y aplicación de la tradición de la protección de las bibliotecas y archivos nacionales en México. In: Sánchez Cordero JA (ed) La Convención de la UNESCO de 1970. Sus nuevos desafíos. Universidad Nacional Autónoma de México, México, pp 57–77

Brunori L (2010) Il nuovo che avanza: Il Museo del Prado e l' "invenzione" di un nuovo regime giuridico fra pubblico e privato. In: Morbidelli G, Cerrina Feroni G (a cura di) I musei. Discipline, gestioni, prospettive. G. Giappichelli Editore, Torino, pp 223–233

Cammelli M (2007) Pubblico e privato nei beni culturali: condizioni di partenza e punti di arrivo. Aedon no 1. http://www.aedon.mulino.it/archivio/2007/1/cammelli.htm

Cammelli M (2011) Capitolo 4: Pluralismo e cooperazione. In: Barbati C, Cammelli M, Sciullo G (a cura di) Diritto e gestione dei beni culturali. Il Mulino, Nuova edizione, pp 175–197

Cano Ruiz I (2012) Patrimonio documental y estatuto Jurídico de los Archivos Eclesiásticos. In: Vega Gutiérrez AM, Martín Garcia M del Mar, Rodríguez Blanco M, Vázquez García-Peñuela JM (coords) Protección del Patrimonio Cultural de Interés Religioso. Actas del V Simposio Internacional de Derecho Concordatario, Logroño, 19–21 de octubre de 2011, Editorial Comares, Granada, pp 177–194

Carnevale R (2010) La Fondazione Preussischer Kulturbesitz (Patrimonio culturale prussiano) e a gestione degli Staatliche Museen zu Berlin (Musei statali di Berlino). In: Morbidelli G, Cerrina

[76] Cerrina Feroni 2010, p. 137.

Feroni G (a cura di) I musei. Discipline, gestioni, prospettive. G. Giappichelli Editore, Torino, pp 235–271
Caruz Arcos E (2009) Principales aspectos de la ordenación jurídica de los museos locales andaluces. Revista de los museos de Andalucía 11:41–45
Cerrina Feroni G (2010) Profili giuridici della gestione dei musei nelle esperienze del Regno Unito, Francia, Germania e Spagna. In: Morbidelli G, Cerrina Feroni G (a cura di) I musei. Discipline, gestioni, prospettive. G. Giappichelli Editore, Torino, pp 81–139
Chizzoniti AG, Margiotta Broglio F (2010) I musei ecclesiastici tra Stato e Chiesa. In: Morbidelli G, Cerrina Feroni G (a cura di) I musei. Discipline, gestioni, prospettive. G. Giappichelli Editore, Torino, pp 141–160
Clarke R (1991) Government policy and art museums in the United Kingdom. In: Feldstein M (ed) The economics of art museums. The University of Chicago Press, Chicago, pp 271–326. http://www.nber.org/chapters/c11645
Clotfelter CT (1991) Government policy toward art museums in the United States. In: Feldstein M (ed) The economics of art museums. The University of Chicago Press, Chicago, pp 237–270. http://www.nber.org/chapters/c11644
Cornu M, Mallet-Poujol N (2006) Droit, oeuvres d'art et musées. Protection et valorisation des collections. CNRS Editions, Paris
Crismani A (2013) I musei tra l'immaginario colletivo e la realta giuridica e gestionale. Aedon, no 3. http://www.aedon.mulino.it/archivio/2013/3/crismani.htm
Denuzzo A (2013). L'ingresso dei musei ecclesiastici nel novero dei beni culturali: alcune riflessioni nella prospettiva del diritto costituzioonale. Stato, Chiese e pluralismo confessionale n 25. www.statoechiese.it/images/stories/2013.7/denuzo_lingresso.pdf
Denuzzo A (2013). La disciplina costituzionale dell'intervento delle fondazioni nel settore museale (e un confronto con l'esperienza tedesca). Aedon, no 3. http://www.aedon.mulino.it/archivio/2013/3/denuzzo.htm
Eccher D (2011) Il nuovo museo. In: Ajani G, Donati A (eds) I diritti dell´arte contemporanea. Umberto Allemandi & C, Torino, pp 79–87
Feliciani G (1998) Autorita ecclesiastiche competenti in materia di beni culturali di interesse religioso. Aedon, no 1. http://www.aedon.mulino.it/archivio/1998/1/felicia.htm
Forte P (2010) Musei e "altri" beni culturali. Codice etico di ICOM e disciplina dei musei in Italia. Aedon, no 2. http://www.aedon.mulino.it/archivio/2010/2/forte.htm
Grailles-Marcilloux B (2013) Archivistiques canadienne et française: échanges, influences ou transferts?. In: Bergeron Y, Frey V (dir) Archives et musées. Le théâtre du patrimoine (France–Canada). Editions du Comité des travaux historiques et scientifiques, pp 47–66
Huo Z (2014) A protracted war: the fight against illicit traffic of cultural property in China. In: Sánchez Cordero JA (ed) La Convención de la UNESCO de 1970. Sus nuevos desafíos. Universidad Nacional Autónoma de México, México, pp 151–174
Litalien R (2013) Les archives éclatées d'une colonisation multiple: un long processus de regroupement. In: Bergeron Y, Frey V (dir) Archives et musées. Le théâtre du patrimoine (France–Canada). Editions du Comité des travaux historiques et scientifiques, pp 33–45
Marcilloux P (2013) Courants d'art: les mouvements de documents et d'œuvres d'art entre la France et le Canada dans les années 1960 et 1970. In: Bergeron Y, Frey V (dir) Archives et musées. Le théâtre du patrimoine (France–Canada). Editions du Comité des travaux historiques et scientifiques, pp 67–78
Moustaira EN (1995) Forum non conveniens. The equity in the frame of legality. Ant. N. Sakkoulas Publications, Athens
Park J (2014) A conceptual framework for analysing social systems surrounding korean national museums in the digital age. In: Proctor N, Cherry R (eds) Museums and the web Asia 2014. Silver Spring (consulted November 9, 2014) http://mwa2014.museumsandtheweb.com/paper/a-conceptual-framework-for-analysing-social-systems-surrounding-korean-national-museums-in-the-digital-age/
Paterson RK (2007) Totems and teapots: the Royal British Columbia Museum Corporation. Univ British Columbia Law Revi 40:421–437

Paterson RK (2013) Museums and the dilemmas of deaccessioning. Transnational Dispute Manage 10(5). www.transnational-dispute-management.com

Pinna G (2005) Patrimonio culturale, musei e il Codice dei beni culturali. Cassanelli R, Pinna G (a cura di) Lo Stato aCulturale. Intorno al Codice dei Beni Culturali. Jaca Book, Milano, pp 41–69

Pinna G (2009–2010) La Europa del sur y sus museos: el caso de Italia. Revista Museos 5–6:68–83

Renna M (2005) I beni museali (privati ed ecclesiastici) nel Codice dei beni culturali e del paesaggio. Aedon, no 1. http://www.aedon.mulino.it/archivio/2005/1/renna.htm

Rosett RN (1991) Art museums in the United States: a financial portrait. In: Feldstein M (ed) The economics of art museums. The University of Chicago Press, Chicago, pp 129–178. http://www.nber.org/chapters/c11641

Sciullo G (2001) Musei e codecisione delle regole. Aedon, no 1. http://www.aedon.mulino.it/archivio/2001/1/sciullo.htm

Settis S (2005) Puo il Museo diventare un'impresa?. In: Settis S (ed) Battaglie senza eroi. I beni culturali tra istituzioni e profitto. Electa per le Belle Arti, Milano, pp 70–78

Severini G (2003) Musei pubblici e musei privati: un genere due specie. Aedon, no 2. http://www.aedon.mulino.it/archivio/2003/2/severini.htm

Stampa A (2007) Modelos de los museos. Panorama legal. Museo 12:19–32

Stampa A (2009) Estrategias, organización y responsabilidad civil en los museos. Revista de los museos de Andalucía 11:52–57

Varutti M (2014) Museums in China: the politics of representation after Mao. The Boydell Press, Woodbridge

Zan L, Bonini Baraldi S (2014) La gestione del patrimonio culturale in Cina: uno sguardo dall'esterno. Aedon no 1. http://www.aedon.mulino.it/archivio/2014/1/zanbonini.htm

Chapter 7
Selling Art—Is it Permitted? And if Yes, Under What Conditions?

7.1 Inalienability

As it is pointed out, "concepts of inalienability, imprescriptibility and indefeasibility, as well as mechanisms such as export control and pre-emption, have served to ensure that the cultural wealth of the nation remains an available resource for its people".[1]

Inalienability of cultural objects is a hot subject for jurists of all countries. It is also "l'objet par excellence" on which a big part of the work of the art historians and the curators is founded.[2]

Different national laws have given in the past[3] and still give different answers to the various questions that could be asked about whether the absolute or nuanced inalienability of cultural objects should be established or whether it should not be foreseen at all.[4]

It is "easier" to speak about the inalienability of the archaeological patrimony, since archaeological objects are considered by most of the countries as a substantive element of the peoples' identity. Inalienability can also offer the best protection to this so vulnerable patrimony.[5]

Can one speak about inalienability of contemporary cultural objects, of "contemporary cultural treasures"? Inalienability is a concept which applies only to

---

[1] Prott 2012, p. 75.

[2] Mairesse 2012, p. 282.

[3] On the history of the concept, specifically in the case of cultural patrimony, see Leniaud 2012, p. 31.

[4] On the private international law issues that arise, see Renold 2012, p. 253.

[5] See Négri 2012, p. 277: "Les caractères du patrimoine archéologique, dont la connaissance n'est pas acquise d'emblée et requiert un processus de mise au jour, lui confèrent une grande vulnérabilité. L'inaliénabilité peut servir la protection de ce patrimoine dont l'intérêt scientifique n'est, le plus souvent, déterminé qu'au moment de sa découverte".

E. Moustaira, *Art Collections, Private and Public: A Comparative Legal Study*,
SpringerBriefs in Law, DOI 10.1007/978-3-319-15802-0_7

public (State) cultural objects, not to those belonging to private persons. In certain cases and under certain conditions, the legislator may end the inalienability of certain cultural objects, without it being considered as contrary to the Constitution.[6]

In order to apply the principle of inalienability, the conditions of its application must be met. This is difficult to happen in the case of contemporary cultural objects, because they cannot really be appreciated as such in the present. Nevertheless, no absolute answer may be given in this as in other issues too, since there are many differences in the various laws regarding the inalienability[7] of cultural objects and its details.

"Res extra commercium" is not the same as inalienability. It means that an object may not become private property.

In Greek law, the inalienability of cultural objects is established since 1899 and it was directly associated to the principle of State's ownership of those cultural goods—archaeological objects, religious objects, but even other cultural objects, those belonging to museums included.[8]

The archaeological collections of Greek museums belong to the State and are res extra commercium. This is the rule for the vast majority of the Hellenic archaeological museums, them being State museums, but also two archaeological museums which recently acquired legal personality of public law and two museums which are private foundations and have archaeological collections (Museum Benaki and Goulandris Museum of Cycladic Art).

The transfer of ownership of State museum objects is not permitted. The only exception to this rule is that on certain conditions and following a certain procedure State museums may exchange for a time period some cultural objects with foreign cultural objects.

Furthermore, the inalienability or limited alienability of collections is foreseen in the statutes of certain museums. Sometimes also, certain cultural objects are donated or legated to museums on the condition not to be alienated by them. The modification of such clauses is only permitted by the Hellenic Constitution on exceptional circumstances (Article 109), when these clauses are parts of donations or testaments done for the profit of public utility aims. It also would be contrary to the mentality of the people who work for the museums.[9]

In Swedish law, there is no legislation specifically regulating museums and their activities, nor are museums prohibited from disposing objects of their collections. Nevertheless, Swedish museums maintain since a long time a strict policy "of not selling or otherwise disposing of items from their collections".[10]

---

[6] Pontier 2012, p. 123.

[7] See Poli 2012, p. 43, speaking about the element of fragility that there is in the concept of inalienability, since it was always admitted, he argues, that a patrimony could not be frozen in all its elements and that it should be allowed to change its status.

[8] Voudouri 2012, p. 53.

[9] Voudouri 2012, pp. 68–69.

[10] Bexhed 2012, p. 165.

This policy, of not selling items of their collections, means that the museums may not dispose them in order either to raise money for operating expenses, or to use the proceeds for investments or new acquisitions for their collections.

German written law, does not know the principle of inalienability (*Unveräußerlichkeit*). It is a concept developed by the German legal theory.[11]

Generally speaking, all cultural goods may be alienated, independently of whether they belong to a private or a public person or whether they are movable or immovable. It is pointed out that there is not a public domain, as there is in other European laws which are founded on the Roman law.

Nevertheless, there are certain special rules for the "public goods". Even those objects, though, are not inalienable. They only are subjected to a special regime, called theory of the modified private property.

According to this theory, which was developed by the German doctrine but is also accepted by the German case law, the rules of that special regime restrict the freedom of the proprietors, as far as the use of the goods is concerned. That is, the proprietors of those goods must respect the public aim, as defined by the public authorities. The moment the public authorities stop insisting on the realization of the public aim, this special regime is terminated.[12]

Inalienability is foreseen by some laws of the *Länder* (*Landesarchivgesetze*) for all the objects that are contained in the public archives. This system, though, is quite complicated, since there are exceptions based on various reasons.

In French law, the concept of inalienability is still important for the law of protection of ownership of the cultural objects, whoever be it their owner. There have been legislative provisions regulating this protection since more than a century. Now they have been codified in the Code de patrimoine.[13]

Article 212-1 states that the public archive are imprescriptible and that no one may possess them without having a legal title and that the private archives which are of public interest because of historic reasons, may be classified as historic archives, sometimes ex officio, by decree of the Conseil d'Etat, becoming thus imprescriptible. This classification does not have inalienability as a consequence, nevertheless, by becoming imprescriptible they cannot be destroyed, consequently they may not be alienated.[14]

The rule that the archives are imprescriptible has as its reason the fact that the archives belong to the movable public domain. Nevertheless, nowhere in the laws' texts is it written that the archives are inalienable.

For the archivists, the absence of the term "inalienable" in the texts concerning the public archives is due to the necessity of proceeding to the elimination of those documents of the archives that have no more administrative of juridical interest.[15]

---

[11] Armbrüster 2012, p. 243.

[12] Armbrüster 2012, p. 245.

[13] Latournerie 2012, pp. 26–27.

[14] Even 2012, p. 149.

[15] Even 2012, p.152.

Interesting is the regulation of the so-called collections of the "France's museums" (*musées de France*):

If the museum belongs to a public entity, the objects that constitute the museum's collection are considered a part of the public domain, thus being inalienable. According to the Article 451-5 of the Code de patrimoine, "every decision about the declassification of these objects may be taken following a consenting opinion of a scientific committee, the composition of which as well as the modalities of its functioning are fixed by decree".[16]

If the musée de France belongs to a non-profit legal entity of private law, the objects of its collection are freely alienable except if they have been acquired by donation or legs or with the aid of the State or of a territorial collectivity. In the latter case, the objects may only be transferred (sold or donated) to public entities or to non-profit private entities that have already promised to respect the fact that these objects constitute part of the public domain. The transfer may only take place after having been approved by the administrative authority.

Movable objects, the conservation of which is of public interest from an art history, science, or technique point of view, are classified by the administrative authority as historic monuments. Article 622-13 of the Code de patrimoine, orders that these movable objects are imprescriptible. Article 622-14 orders that objects classified as historic monuments belonging to the State are inalienable and that those belonging to a territorial collectivity or to a public entity or an entity of public utility may only be alienated following a consenting opinion of the administrative authority.

7.1.1 A "Strange" Case: Korean Royal Archives as French Cultural Property?...

In 1866, the French navy invaded Korea—the reason presented was the massacre of 9 French priests and many Christian Koreans—and took 297 volumes of Korean royal archives from the Joseon Dynasty (1392–1910),[17] which were in the Outer Gyujang-gak Library, known as Oe-Gyujang-gak, on the Ganghwa Island, near Seoul at the mouth of the Han River. This library was built to accommodate the overflow of books from the main Gyujang-gak Library at Changdeok Palace.[18]

---

[16] As it is stated, the inalienability of collections has been used as an argument in several cases in which French museums were involved—mostly concerning human remains and sovereign archives, which the museums did not want to restitute claiming that they belonged to the public domain and therefore they were inalienable, see Cornu and Renold 2010, p. 9 and the case, infra, 7.1.1.

[17] About the evolution of law in Korea from the Joseon dynasty through the colonial and post-colonial periods, see Seong-Hak Kim 2012.

[18] Song-Mi 2008, p. 114.

The manuscripts were official records of a government committee responsible for planning special state events and rituals for the royalty—they are known as Uigwe.[19] As it is stated, in these manuscripts one can retrieve information on, among others, "Joseon society, politics, economics, rituals, literature, art history, musicology, culinary history".[20]

Right after having been seized, the 297 manuscripts were expedited to France and "donated" to the Bibliothèque Nationale de France (BnF), in 1867. For more than a century they stayed there, unnoticed.[21]

In 1975, they were "discovered" in the stockroom that BnF had in Versailles—they were mentioned as "Chinese" works. In 1991, Professors of the Seoul University asked the Korean government to start negotiations about the manuscripts' restitution. The Korean government did that, but for many years nothing much happened—only in 1993, President Mitterand decided the restitution to South Korea of one(!) of these manuscripts. It was supposed to be a goodwill gesture. At that time France was competing for a large contract for high-speed rail in South Korea and ultimately won it.[22]

The most "strange" in this case was that on 18 December 2009, a French administrative tribunal (*Tribunal administratif de Paris*) found that the seized Korean archives constituted inalienable French property. That was the stance that generally France kept, as far as that kind of treasures once taken away by force and ever since in its territory is concerned.

Knowing that already, it was a Korean cultural organization ("Cultural Action") that had taken the initiative to file an action, in 2008, before the French tribunal, after having received a negative answer from the French Minister of Culture on its petition that he undertake efforts to have the archives declassified as French property.

Thus, Cultural Action sought an order from the French administrative tribunal, in which the tribunal would "acknowledge, principally, that the royal archives are not part of the property of the public domain of the French government" or, in the alternative, would set aside the Minister's earlier refusal and would "direct the regulatory authorities to submit a bill before Parliament for purposes of declassification from the French public domain of the Korean Royal Archives".[23]

---

[19] In 2007, more than 3,000 Uigwe volumes were inscribed in UNESCO's Memory of the World register. The nomination applied to Uigwe manuscripts in South Korea custody, but it also noted the existence of the additional 297 volumes "taken from Oeguyanggak (the Ganghwa-do branch of the Royal library Kyujanggak of Joseon) during the invasion of Ganghwa-do by a French fleet in 1866", UNESCO. *Uigwe: The Royal Protocols of the Joseon Dynasty*, http://www.unesco.org/new/en/communication-and-information/flagship-project-activities/memory-of-the-world/register/full-list-of-registered-heritage/registered-heritage-page-9/uigwe-the-royal-protocols-of-the-joseon-dynasty/#c191886 (2007).

[20] Song-Mi 2008, p. 114.

[21] Cox 2011-A, p. 409.

[22] Cox 2011-A, p. 413.

[23] Cox 2011-A, p. 414.

The French tribunal rejected all the arguments of Cultural Action:

- It held that Korean laws that protect the Korean cultural heritage were "irrelevant" to the French proceedings.
- It rejected the applicability of the 1954 Hague Convention on the Protection of Cultural Property in the Event of Armed Conflict and of the 1970 UNESCO Convention on the Means of Prohibiting and Preventing the Illicit Import, Export and Transfer of Ownership of Cultural Property, on the ground that neither of them was retroactive.
- It rejected the applicability of the 1995 UNIDROIT Convention on Stolen or Illegally Exported Cultural Objects, on the ground that France was not a party.
- In addressing the argument of Cultural Action, that the lack of connection between the Korean royal archives and France prevented them from qualifying as France's "public property", the tribunal stated that it had not been disputed that the documents within the BnF had been from the beginning dedicated to the public use. Furthermore, it stated that, regardless of the circumstances of their initial seizure, they had become part of the French public domain, having been held by BnF for 140 years and thus being accessible to the public.

One may really wonder about the ethics of the latter statement.

- To the arguments of Cultural Action that according to principles of international customary law[24] the looted royal archives should be restituted to South Korea, the French tribunal concluded that "in any event" there could not be established that there was such an international custom at that time (19th century).[25]

As it is pointed out, the French decision relied in part on the fact that the 1,866 royal documents' seizure took place before the 1907 and 1954 Hague Conventions which regulate this issue; that is, during a time when seizure of enemy property was not really rare. However, the result in this case has many similarities to what happened in more modern conflict cases.

Thus, it is sadly interesting that even following the evolution of both the international treaty law and the international customary law, which require the restitution of captured sovereign documents during armed conflicts,[26] this does not necessarily happens. For example,[27] when USA decided to give seized records back

---

[24] Three specific historical peace treaties were cited: the Treaty of Paris in 1814, the Treaty of Vienna in 1864, and the Treaty between Prussia and the Grand Duchy of Hesse in 1866.

[25] Cox 2011-A, pp. 414–416.

[26] See also Cornu and Renold 2010, p. 17, that the Korean archives "might be returned to their country of origin, as they are genuine sovereign archives, founding documents that are essential to an understanding of present-day Korea".

[27] Stated by Cox 2011-B, p. 465.

to Germany following World War II, it made clear that "legal title" to at least some seized records was "held by the United States Government" and that those records would be "donated" to Germany.[28]

In June 2011, France gave the manuscripts back to South Korea, though not restituting their ownership, but only as a 5-year renewable loan.

7.2 De-accessioning

Certain museums in common law countries are subject to statutory prohibitions on divestment or *de-accessioning*. There are differences between inalienability and prohibitions on divestment, the two concepts are not equivalent.

Deaccession is not a term of art in the legal sense, nevertheless it is a term commonly used in the museum world[29] and it means the administrative removal of an artwork from a collection,[30] which is usually followed by "the voluntary sale of objects for value based on a perceived need on the part of the selling institution for the funds generated by the sale".[31]

According to New York Education Law § 233-a(1)(b), deaccession of art is: "the permanent removal or disposal of an object from the collection of the museum by virtue of its sale, exchange, donation or transfer by any means to any person".

Inalienability has as a consequence the invalidation of subsequent transactions, even where the purchaser is of good faith. Statutory prohibitions—if and when they exist—on divestment are directed to the trustees of the museums. The trustees are liable for breach of trust, but the transactions are not invalidated.

In November 2007, the Association of Art Museum Directors, an organization representing over 190 directors of the major art museums in the USA, Canada and Mexico, issued a report entitled: "Art Museums and the Practice of Deaccessioning". In June 2010, the report was revised.

According to this report, deaccessioning is defined as the process by which an artwork, wholly or in part, is permanently removed from a museum's collection. Disposal is defined as the transfer of ownership of the artwork by the museum, after

---

[28] General Records Schedule, "Seized German Records", 1 August 1953, National Archives, Record Group 242, Pomerenze Collection, AGAR-S No.3144, http://www.dcoxfiles.com/3144.pdf.

[29] As Fincham 2011, p. 2 states, the term 'deaccession' was first used in an article of New York Times, in 1972, by the arts critic John Canaday ("Very Quiet and Very Dangerous", *New York Times*, 27 February 1972), who expressed his concerns over a quiet sale by the Museum of Modern Art, which had 'recently de-accessioned (the polite term for "sold") one of its only four Redons, the gift of a prominent collector, rechanneling it into private hands—another prominent collector—by way of a dealer.'

[30] Simpson 2008, states that others insist that the term includes both the administrative removal of the artwork from the collection and its disposal. According to his view, though, the two procedures are different, with different risks and different purposes.

[31] Paterson 2013.

this artwork has been deaccessioned. In the case of false or fraudulent works, or in the case of artworks that have been irreparably damaged or cannot practically be restore, disposal means removal from the collection and disposition as determined by the museum, destruction of the artwork included.[32]

As it is stated, the practice of deaccessioning is one of the most controversial aspects of museum governance, one of the "most debated and sensitive issues for museums today".[33] It is often viewed more as an ethical issue than a legal one.[34]

7.2.1 Arguments for and Against Deacccessioning

The arguments put forth in favor of undertaking deaccessioning are the following:

- The improvement of collection, since the cost of administering, storing, securing and conserving the collection is high and it is difficult for the museums both to face it and to add more artworks to the collection.[35]
- The function of the collection, since some collection material had been acquired for research programs, therefore it had been accessioned "in the knowledge and expectation that it would, one day, be deaccessioned".
- The change of collection function, since the focus of museums and art galleries is not anymore in the collecting procedure, but has been moved to the public access and exhibition. Consequently, it is argued, they need fewer artworks but of greater quality or greater public interest.
- Application of governing rules, since for some types of collections, as for example government archives, deaccession is mandated by legislation.

The arguments put forth against deaccessioning are the following:

- The existence of Acts or regulations or administrative directives limiting or prohibiting totally or partially deaccessioning.
- There may me forbiddances of transactions, such as preconditions imposed on gifts and bequests or certain trust arrangements—for example, a gift of collection, with restrictions against dividing or selling the collection.
- Given the fact that each work is the unique expression of its creator, one cannot speak about superior or inferior works of art, therefore any deaccessioning would not only by inappropriate but it would also be unethical.
- There have been examples of deaccessioning artworks by museums following a certain "fashion", which subsequenty was proved totally wrong.

---

[32] Report of the Association of Art Museums Directors, "AAMD Policy on Deaccessioning", June 9, 2010, http://aamd.org/papers/documents/FinalDeaccessioning_Report_6_25_10.pdf.

[33] Tam 2012, p. 852.

[34] Howard 2012, p. 206.

[35] Goldstein 1997, p. 213.

- In case of works of living artists, deaccessioning would be very dangerous for the "value" of their works, as recognized by the art market.
- Deaccessioning could damage the relationships of the museums with the donors.
- Sometimes the deaccessioning is serving purposes other than the enrichment of the museum's collection: for example, the money obtained is used for purposes of construction or renovation or administration.[36]

Indeed, even the adherents to a deaccession policy admit that it is an at least difficult issue.[37] Sometimes they try to put the blame on "a regrettable negligence of scholarly literature", arguing that while academia has given sufficient reasons for the existence of deaccessioning, it has clarified whether that could be a solution to museums' resource problems.[38]

7.2.2 Deaccessioning in USA and in United Kingdom

In the USA museum world, deaccessioning for the purpose of selling art for operating expenses[39] is an unthinkable transgression.[40] However, until now no state has enacted any statute restricting deaccession. Only some states put certain requirements before deaccession, attempting thus to regulate it.[41]

That means that museums may deaccession artworks freely in most cases, except if and when such artworks have been donated with conditions or when the sale violates a fiduciary's duty of loyalty or due care.[42] When a donor attaches restrictions on the gift, the museum is obliged to respect them,[43] except if a court in equity allows a museum to sell the object of the gift, by reforming the gift instrument under the doctrine of *cy pres*.[44] Donor restrictions on charitable gifts can remain effective forever. Limiting provisions, such as the Rule against Perpetuities, do not apply to these gifts.[45]

---

36 Simpson 2008.

37 Orloski 2008, p. 605.

38 Vecco and Piazzai 2014.

39 White 1995, pp. 1065–1066, was arguing that if the trustees keep the trust standard of conduct, museums should be permitted to deaccession to raise operating funds.

40 Sugin 2010, p. 102.

41 Fincham 2011, p. 9.

42 Gerstenblith 2003, p. 409.

43 Varson Cromer 2006, p. 780.

44 See Fincham 2011, p. 14, who states that *cy pres* allows a court in equity to amend the terms of a charitable gift if the terms are impractical, illegal or impossible to effectuate and if the donor had a general charitable intent.

45 Gerstenblith 1983, p. 179.

An interesting argument that has been put forth against deaccessioning is that museums keep artworks for the public trust. This means that the museum community has obligations towards its public.

The doctrine of public trust has been used in property and environmental law, in order to avoid the exploitation of natural resources and provide standing for citizens to ask for environmental protection.[46] Although this doctrine has been applied to artworks in many cases,[47] rare are the scholars who have done a deep research about how it could be used as a tool in art and cultural heritage law. One among those has argued that artworks which become parts of museum collections cannot later go back to private ownership; and that if they had to be sold only other public institutions should be permitted to buy them.[48]

This doctrine originates in the Roman concept of public property, according to which, certain parts of the environment could not be subject to private ownership; on the contrary, they were dedicated for public use. This doctrine has been adopted by the civil law of many continental countries in Europe but also by the common law in England, where the public trust doctrine was incorporated into the Magna Carta. This doctrine[49] is the root of the provisions in many national laws in respect of cultural heritage, which provisions restrict or forbid the private ownership of certain objects and restrict or forbid their exportation.

During the economic recession that followed the defaults of 2008, several museums in USA faced big financial difficulties. Some of them did not make it, some of them were rescued at the last moment.

In New York City, the American Folk Art Museum, a 50-year-old museum and "the world's center of folk-outsider art", defaulted on a $31.9 million loan taken out in 2009. It had used the money of the loan to build a new flagship site. After defaulting, at the beginning of 2011 it was contemplating closing down, refusing to sell works to pay the debt. One month later, it was rescued by pledges of donations from trustees and from the Ford Foundation.

Some U.S. museums, struggling to survive, proceeded to deaccessionning and sale of paintings of their collections[50]—in one case, there was even a proposal to sell the whole collection of a museum.[51]

---

[46] Fincham 2011, p. 22.

[47] Porges 1981, p. 135. She argues that the public trust doctrine offers a legal theory for the protection of artworks.

[48] Gerstenblith 1983, pp. 192–193.

[49] Which gained widespread attention in USA, after a decision by the Supreme Court in 1892, in the case *Illinois Central Railroad v. Illinois*, 146 U.S. 387 (1892).

[50] That—a museum wishing to sell objects to raise funds to meet financial obligations—is one of the three general contexts in which the small but growing number of cases have addressed a trustee's or director's actions, as Fincham 2011, p. 6 states. The other two are: "when museums undertake a sale and use the proceeds to make capital improvements" and "when a sale involves a sale to a museum trustee (and may be considered self-dealing) or if a sale price falls below market value".

[51] Ackers Cirigliana 2011, pp. 368–372.

In order to stop such movements, considered as "unethical",[52] a bill was introduced into the New York state legislation, in 2009, according to which all sales of artworks to cover operating expenses by state cultural institutions would be illegal.[53] This bill "would have been the first comprehensive legislation targeting the perceived problems surrounding deaccessioning".[54] Finally, it was not approved.

It must be pointed out that in USA, some museums have defined a specific internal deaccessioning policy.[55]

In the United Kingdom, powers of de-accession are discretionary, and they may be exercised in accordance with policies voluntarily adopted by each museum or gallery.

Discussion about the desirability of de-accession had started there in 1962, when "fears for the sale in the open market of Leonardo's cartoon of "The Virgin and Child with St. John the Baptist and St. Anne" had led to the appointment of the Cottesloe Committee".

The report of the Committee was published in 1964, proposing legislation according to which the governmental consent would be required for the sale of "important" works of art owned by the Government and the Reviewing Committee should give her approval for the exportation of artworks the value of which would be more than 25,000 pounds.

Again, in the early Nineties similar recommendations were advanced in a report, following sales of important artworks by two English museums. Both reports were ignored.[56]

The legal treatment of de-accessioning in UK differs across the categories of collection recognized by law. Different rules apply across England, Wales, Northern Ireland and Scotland.[57]

"Local collections"—collections held by autonomous local government authorities[58]—are regulated in England and Wales by Public Libraries and Museums Act 1964, in which there is no prohibition against de-accession.

Unless it can be proved that a local collection is subject to a private trust obligation prohibiting de-accession, the mayor and the elected council may sell some artworks or the whole collection, if they think that this would be in the interest of the inhabitants of their area.[59] This wide discretion was recognized by the UK museum community at about the late 1990s.

---

[52] An important case in which the ethical implications of deaccessioning were discussed, was the one concerning the Barnes Foundation. The court held that there was not an absolute prohibition, see *In re the Barnes Foundation*, 24 Fiduc.Rep. 2d 94, Court of Common Pleas of Montgomery County, Pennsylvania Orphans' Court, 2004; *In re the Barnes Foundation*, Orphans' Court, 2004, 69 Pa.D.& C.4th 129.

[53] Assemb. B.6959-A, 232 Sess. (N.Y. 2009).

[54] Paterson 2013.

[55] Pizzi 2011, pp. 128–129.

[56] Crivellaro 2011.

[57] Doubleday 2012, p. 178.

[58] Local Government Act 1972, Section 139.

[59] Local Government Act, Section 111.

According to the Scottish law, local museums may sell or exchange works of art only if they are duplicates.[60] According to the Northern Ireland Law, local authorities may make their own byelaws for the governance of their collections.[61]

All national collections in England and Scotland, most university collections and the National Museum of Wales are "charitable collections".[62] Museums are the owners of objects for their charitable purposes and for public benefit. According to the Charities Act 2006, Section 2(1)(f), among the charitable purposes are "the advancement of arts, culture, heritage and science". Therefore, museums are prohibited from de-accessioning their collections, because they are responsible in law to keep and display them.

In some charity foundation documents there are express prohibitions, either absolute or conditional, against the disposal of the collection's objects. If there is no express provision in those documents, a charitable museum cannot de-accession the objects of its collection without the authority of the courts, the Charity Commissioners or the Attorney General.[63]

"Private trust collections" are those collections which are subject to private trust conditions, imposed by deed of gift or by a will. Usually these conditions limit the powers of museums to de-accession.

Specifically certain UK museums—such as the British Museum, the National Portrait Gallery, the Tate Gallery, the Victoria and Albert Museum, the British Library, etc., constituting national collections, that is, charitable collections created by Acts of Parliament, have to follow strict rules about holding their collections in perpetuity. They only may de-accession in very specific circumstances and as an exception to the rule, which is to be retained for the benefit of museum visitors now and in the future.

Between 1753 (when the British Museum was founded[64]) and 1992 (year of issue of the Museums and Galleries Act), the Parliament had given to the trustees of each museum or gallery those powers of disposal that they needed for the better governance of their collections and for fulfilling their charitable obligations.

Section 6 of the Museums and Galleries Act 1992 gives national museums the power to transfer artworks between themselves. A provision is included, according to which, an artwork that is subject to private trust obligations cannot be moved from one national museum to another without the consent of the donor who might have originally required that the artwork be held in a specific national museum and not be moved to some other.[65]

---

[60] Public Libraries Consolidation (Scotland) Act 1887, s. 21, and Education (Scotland) Act.

[61] Museums and Galleries (Northern Ireland) Order 1998, Article 13.

[62] Charities Acat 1993, Section 3 and schedule 2.

[63] Doubleday 2012, pp. 179–180.

[64] The 1753 Act created a charitable obligation that the collection was to be "preserved and maintained, not only for the Inspection and Entertainment of the learned and the curious, but for the general Use and Benefit of the Public".

[65] Doubleday 2012, p. 184.

Procedures adapted to the mentality of the common law systems are almost always ill-suited for other countries, for other legal cultures.[66] Even less so, when these procedures are causing heated debates on their desirability or on their ethical standards, as deaccessioning is.

U.S. museums are “mostly funded by private donations and self-generated income”. Their “collections consist principally of objects donated by collectors or purchased with monetary gifts and bequests from collectors and other private players and supporters”.[67] Would the deaccessioning procedure be accepted by the law governing museums in European countries, where the public entity dimension of cultural institutions is very much stressed? It is really doubtful, since most of the jurists who write about it are either critical or even hostile.

References

Armbrüster C (2012) L'inaliénabilté en droit allemand. In: Cornu M, Fromageau J, Poli J-F, Taylor A-C (dir) L'inaliénabilité des collections, performances et limites? L' Harmattan, Paris, pp 243–250

Bexhed J-M (2012) L'inaliénabilité dans les pays du Nord. In: Cornu M, Fromageau J, Poli J-F, Taylor A-C (dir) L'inaliénabilité des collections, performances et limites? L' Harmattan, Paris, pp 157–166

Cirigliana J (2011) Let them sell art: why a broader deaccession policy today could save museums tomorrow. S Calif Interdisc Law J 20:365–393

Cornu M, Renold M-A (2010) New developments in the restitution of cultural property: alternative means of dispute resolution. Int J Cult Prop 17:1–31

Cox D (2011a) “Inalienable” archives: Korean royal archives as French property under international law. Int J Cult Prop 18:409–423

Cox D (2011b) National archives and international conflicts: the society of American archivists and war. Am Archivist 74:451–481

Crivellaro J (2011) The politics of deaccession: English and American insight into the disposition of artworks from museums. Aedon no 3. http://www.aedon.mulino.it/archivio/2011/3/crivellaro.htm

Doubleday T (2012) Legal powers and prohibitions on de-accessioning affecting museums and galleries in the UK. In: Cornu M, Fromageau J, Poli J-F, Taylor A-C (dir) L'inaliénabilité des collections, performances et limites? L' Harmattan, Paris, pp 177–191

Even P (2012) Inaliénabilité et archives publiques. In: Cornu M, Fromageau J, Poli J-F, Taylor A-C (dir) L'inaliénabilité des collections, performances et limites? L' Harmattan, Paris, pp 145–155

Fincham D (2011) Deaccession of art from the public trust. Art Antiq Law 16:1–37

Gerstenblith P (1983) The fiduciary duties of museum trustees. 8 Columbia J Law Arts 8:175–206

Gerstenblith P (2003) Acquisition and deacquisition of museum collections and the fiduciary obligations of museums to the public. Cardozo J Int Comp Law 11:409–465

Goldstein JR (1997) Deaccession: not such a dirty word. Cardozo Arts Entertain Law J 15:213–247

[66] Crivellaro 2011.

[67] Merryman 2009.

Howard K (2012) Deaccessioning—rules and practices at United States art museums. In: Cornu M, Fromageau J, Poli J-F, Taylor A-C (dir) L'inaliénabilité des collections, performances et limites? L' Harmattan, Paris, pp 205–241

Latournerie M-A (2012) L'inaliénabilité, histoire d'un concept du point de vue de l'histoire du droit. In: Cornu M, Fromageau J, Poli J-F, Taylor A-C (dir) L'inaliénabilité des collections, performances et limites? L' Harmattan, Paris, pp 11–30

Leniaud J-M (2012) L'inaliénabilité: histoire d'un concept du point de vue de l'histoire du patrimoine. In: Cornu M, Fromageau J, Poli J-F, Taylor A-C (dir) L'inaliénabilité des collections, performances et limites? L' Harmattan, Paris, pp 31–38

Mairesse F (2012) L'aliénation entre raison et passion. In: Cornu M, Fromageau J, Poli J-F, Taylor A-C (dir) L'inaliénabilité des collections, performances et limites? L' Harmattan, Paris, pp 281–298

Merryman J H (2009) Art systems and cultural policy. Stanford public law working paper no 1489612. http://ssrn.com/abstract=1489612

Négri V (2012) Sur l'inaliénabilité du patrimoine archéologique. In: Cornu M, Fromageau J, Poli J-F, Taylor A-C (dir) L'inaliénabilité des collections, performances et limites? L' Harmattan, Paris, pp 267–279

Orloski M (2008) Preventing gross injury to local cultural patrimony: a proposal for state regulation of deaccessioning. Temple Law Rev 81:605–634

Paterson RK (2013) Museums and the dilemmas of deaccessioning. Transnational Dispute Manage 10(5) www.transnational-dispute-management.com

Pizzi A (2011) Alcune considerazioni in materia di deaccessioning delle collezioni dei musei; writing e diritto d'autore; restauro dell'arte contemporanea. In: Ajani G, Donati A (ed) I diritti dell'arte contemporanea. Umberto Allemandi and C, Torino, pp 127–137

Poli J-F (2012) Les fondements de la règle de l'inaliénabilité dans le droit du patrimoine culturel. In: Cornu M, Fromageau J, Poli J-F, Taylor A-C (dir) L'inaliénabilité des collections, performances et limites? L' Harmattan, Paris, pp 41–52

Pontier J-M (2012) La question de l'inaliénabilité appliquée au patrimoine contemporain. In: Cornu M, Fromageau J, Poli J-F, Taylor A-C (dir) L'inaliénabilité des collections, performances et limites? L' Harmattan, Paris, pp 121–143

Porges ER (1981) Protecting the public interest in art. Yale Law J 91:121–167

Prott LV (2012) Inalienability and other modes of protection in current legal systems. In: Cornu M, Fromageau J, Poli J-F, Taylor A-C (dir) L'inaliénabilité des collections, performances et limites? L' Harmattan, Paris, pp 75–101

Renold M-A (2012) Inaliénabilité de biens culturels et territorialité: l'approche du droit international privé. In: Cornu M, Fromageau J, Poli J-F, Taylor A-C (dir) L'inaliénabilité des collections, performances et limites? L' Harmattan, Paris, pp 253–265

Seong-Hak Kim M (2012) Law and custom in Korea. Comparative legal history. Cambridge University Press, New York

Simpson S (2008) Collections law. Legal issues for Australian archives, galleries, libraries and museums (Chapter 8. Deaccessioning of material from the collection). http://www.collectionslaw.com.au

Song-Mi Y (2008) Euigwe and the documentation of Joseon court ritual life. Arch Asian Art 58:113–133

Sugin L (2010) Lifting the museum's burden from the backs of the university: should the art collection be treated as part of the endowment? N Engl Law Rev 44:541–579

Tam S (2012) In museums we trust: analyzing the mission of museums, deaccessioning policies, and the public trust. Fordham Urban Law J 39:849–901

Varson Cromer M (2006) Don't give me that!: tax valuation of gifts to art museums. Washington Lee Law Rev 63:777–808

Vecco M, Piazzai M (2014) Deaccessioning of museums collections: what do we know and where do we stand in Europe? J Cult Heritage. http://dx.doi.org/10.1016/j.culher.2014.03.007

Voudouri D (2012) L'inaliénabiité comme mode de protection du patrimoine culturel en Grèce. In: Cornu M, Fromageau J, Poli J-F, Taylor A-C (dir) L'inaliénabilité des collections, performances et limites? L' Harmattan, Paris, pp 53–72

White JL (1995) When it's ok to sell the monet: a trustee-fiduciary-duty framework for analyzing the deaccessioning of art to meet museum operating expenses. Michigan Law Rev 94:1041–1066

Chapter 8
Cultural Economics

8.1 General Comments

During the last decades of the 20th century a "new science" has been developed: Cultural Economics. A child of time, it reflects the changing mentality about art collecting which, from a distinguished occupation mostly moving around cultural choices, has also become a set of economic choices, putting art works in the framework of a series of investment products.

Both cultural value and economic value, it is argued, are socially constructed measures. Both are accessible to observation.[1] Culture and economics could be approached in two ways, according to the supporters of an existing relationship between them. The first approach would be to study exactly this relationship, while the second approach would be to study the arts with the help of economic analysis.[2]

Cultural Economics or Arts' Economics focuses on economic studies of arts that include a wide range of cultural objects' issues, such as the conservation of historic and artistic cultural property/heritage or the protection of paintings or plastic arts.[3]

8.2 Museums Between Private and Public—The Beyeler Museum

Some large and important private collections are not completely private since they receive public support, becoming museums. In the past, such private collections would probably have been donated to some public organizations, while now they prefer to form part or the whole of privately founded museums.

[1] Hutter and Frey 2010, p. 36.
[2] Frey 2009.
[3] Pérez-Bustamante Yábar 2008, p. 193.

E. Moustaira, *Art Collections, Private and Public: A Comparative Legal Study*,
SpringerBriefs in Law, DOI 10.1007/978-3-319-15802-0_8

The number of these museums is growing, it seems. The supporters of cultural economics' approaches consider these museums as a very interesting object of study, a "testing ground for an institutionally based economic theory of museums". Thus, they attempt to analyze how this dual nature—privately founded art museum receiving public support—influences "the museum's behavior".

Such a study is the one concerning "The Beyeler Museum" in Basle, Switzerland, focusing on three aspects: (1) the relationship of the collection to special exhibitions; (2) how much the museum relies on the market; and (3) the amenities for visitors.[4]

The Beyeler Museum[5] is located in Riehen, canton Basle, and it was founded in 1997 by an art dealer, Ernst Beyeler, in order to host 170 works of Classical Modern art.

The analysis made of the museum's case applies economic thinking to the arts, using the economic model of human behavior; an approach very different from that taken by other social sciences or the art history. The "problem" here is that the examples used are almost exclusively museums in USA.

Starting with the main actors of a museum, that is, the directorate and the professional staff, the study prefers to limit itself to the directorate. In order to explain the behavior of the museum directorate, it seeks the circumstances they are working in and the problems that they must face. Obviously, the available finances, the available budget are the most important constraint the directorate must face. Some depend mostly on public grants, while others depend exclusively on private money, that is, the funding of museums is heterogeneous.[6]

Directors of public museums rely exclusively on public grants. According to this analysis, this fact provides little incentive to get additional income and to achieve minimum costs, with the consequences that (a) public museums distance themselves completely from the art market, (b) directors are less interested in the number of visitors, and (c) the visitors' amenities are poorly developed.

On the contrary, according to this analysis, directors of private museums have strong incentives to get additional income, with the consequences that (a) private museums rely on the market, (b) they are more concerned with attracting visitors, and (c) they emphasize the amenities for visitors.[7]

Based on the above thoughts, the study applies them to the Museum Beyeler case. The canton Basle-Stadt and the Riehen Commune grant a subsidy of 1.75 million Swiss Francs per year for the first 10 years of operation, as well as the use of the park for 80 years.[8] As far as the latter is concerned, it should be clarified that the land on which the Museum is built and the administrative buildings of the museum

---

4 Frey and Meier 2002.

5 www.beyeler.com.

6 Rosett 1991, p. 129.

7 Frey and Meier 2002.

8 Granting the use of the park was sanctioned by the Commune of Riehen citizens' vote, in June 1993, by a large majority of the voters: 60.8 % were in favor, with a participation rate of 67.4 %.

are provided to the museum free of charge by the Commune of Riehen, but remain the Commune's property.

The museum receives public grants at 14–22 % of its budget. All the additional income must be earned by the museum itself. The deficits are paid by the founder Ernst Beyeler.[9]

It is very interesting that, contrary to what one would wait, the museum's collection policy distances itself from the art market. This is made clear by the following:

Article 3 of the contract with the state, following which the museum receives fixed subsidies for a period of 10 years, contains a clause prohibiting the sale of the collection during the period of the subsidy. Ernst Beyeler is still maintaining his gallery, but separates clearly the activities of the museum from the commercial activities of the gallery.

The museum does not publish in its balance sheet the value of the collection as its main asset. This is what all museums usually do and, according to the study, it is not really what should be done, since museums "tend to undervalue potential losses and overvalue benefits".[10]

As far as its lending policy is concerned, the Beyeler Museum is very strict and it only lends artworks in exchange for other museums' artworks and not for money, refraining thus from pricing the artworks.

The study is somewhat severe on the results of the special exhibitions that the Beyeler museum mounts, arguing that many of them "could have been organized perhaps equally well by other institutions". Among its conclusions is that the Beyeler Museum has proved that "intermediate forms of governance between private and public" may work extremely well. Nevertheless, according to the (too much imbued in the "law and economics" theory) study, this "happy marriage" might not be sustainable in the long run.[11]

8.3 The Collector as Factor of Art Objects' Market Value's Construction

The collector may be considered as one of the three categories of economic subjects that intervene in the art market—the other two being the artists and the galleries.

More than in other cases, in the art market the demand influences in an unequal manner the money value of the artworks and the choices of the buyers determine substantially the viability and the sustainability of a certain art production. This is due to the fact that for various reasons—among them, the particular relation

[9] After the founder's death, no other person will be 'liable' for potential losses and this, according to the study, weakens the incentives that the museum will have to be financially successful.

[10] Frey and Meier 2002.

[11] Frey and Meier 2002.

established in this type of objects between the use value and the exchange value as well as the instable character of the critiques on the contemporary art—it is a market that shows a tendency to speculation.

This characteristic, together with the faint relation between the cost of production of an art work and its price, have led people to compare it with the stock market.

Nevertheless, as it is argued, this comparison has nothing to do with reality, insofar as the art objects are unique, something that makes it even more difficult to establish a unifying equivalence between them. While the objective value of the stock market shares is the dividend that these may supply, in the case of art objects the objective factor is the esthetic valorization. Thus, the objectivity of the latter depends on the socially constructed and constantly disputed legitimacy.[12]

It could be supported, that the economic value of a unique piece of artwork depends, at the same time, on an "inherently subjective process"[13] and on an objective aesthetic value. It might be the so called "handshake agreement" culture of the art world.[14]

According to a specific survey that has used empirical analysis of information on private art collections all over the world, most private collections are located in Europe, North America and Asia, while there are relatively few such collections in Latin America and even fewer in Africa.

Conducting this survey, it has been observed that there is a strong home bias in private art collections. This well-known in finance phenomenon, that means that financial investors tend to invest many of their assets into corporations located in their own country even if that means a lower rate of return, may also be observed in other markets, art market included.

Thus, according to this survey, collectors tend to acquire art objects related to their own country, feeling a special attachment to "artists sharing the same culture, history and nationality and whom they sometimes know personally".[15] Another reason for this home bias, according to the same survey, is the legal barriers restricting international transactions, that is, import and export restrictions imposed by countries.

8.4 Growth of Art Market Around the World

As it has been pointed out, since the decade of 1950 the art market has been dominated by art sales in USA and in United Kingdom. In 2011, the geographic distribution was shuttered, being China the country that occupied the first seat in terms of national value of sales in auction houses and galleries.

---

[12] Cerviño 2011.

[13] Steinkamp 1994, p. 338.

[14] Jay 2009, pp. 1860–1862.

[15] Steiner et al. 2013.

Some years ago, an explanation offered about the growth of the art market around the world, stated as reasons: the enormous liquidity of the economic system, the appearance of specialized inversion funds, the social consideration among the collecting elite, the appearance for the first time of collectors from certain countries, such as Russia and China, as well as the consolidation of the U.S. art market, of which the art collectors are the actual buyers of about 50 % of the art works. Another reason that could be added is the first appearance not only of art collectors from countries or regions of the world until then ignored as far as art circulation is concerned, but also of artworks originated in these countries/regions—as, for example, Asian, Latin American, or Russian.[16]

In Europe, it seems that the strongest countries in this section are United Kingdom, France, Italy and Germany. Right after them, are classified Spain, Austria, Switzerland, Netherlands and Belgium.[17] According to the previously mentioned survey, about the collectors' home bias, the ten countries holding the most collections are: United States, Germany, United Kingdom, China, Brazil, South Korea, Spain, Italy, France, India.[18]

8.5 National Art Markets

In Spain, according to a survey of 2012, there are 125 auction houses, which sell antiquities and pieces of contemporary art. There are also offices of the two international auction houses Christie's and Sotheby's, which have not performed any auctions since 2008, though.

The Spanish auction houses realize their sales via pubic auctions, private sales and online sales. Contrary to what happens in United Kingdom or USA, or other important art markets, where the most expensive art objects are being sold in public auctions, in Spain these objects most usually are being sold via private sales. The online sales are important enough in Spain, since they represent about 13 % of the sales of art objects.

The art galleries are about 3,500—either of antiquities or modern and contemporary art (most of them) or decorative art. 600 of these galleries realize about 70 % of all galleries' sales.[19] Most of them are focused in national market, while others are internationally oriented. Contrary to what happens in auction houses, galleries realize only 5 % of their sales online.

[16] Barraca de Ramos 2008, p. 64.

[17] McAndrew 2012, p. 16.

[18] Steiner et al. 2013.

[19] McAndrew 2012, pp. 21–29.

8.6 Authenticity of Artworks

Artworks are often sold for huge sums. The buyers—usually collectors—want to be sure about the authenticity of the artworks they buy, since it could not be excluded that these items are fakes or that they have been forged, or misattributed or reattributed.

"Can the principle of caveat emptor (buyer beware) apply to issues of appraisal and authentication in the largely unregulated art market?", it is asked.[20] This is a question put by a U.S. scholar, regarding U.S. law, but obviously a question about the liability of art experts may concern all national laws.

As it is pointed out, in USA an appraisal is not by itself a warranty of authenticity, under the Uniform Commercial Code. Nevertheless, when one donates [art] property and submits an appraisal to the Internal Revenue Service (IRS) for purposes of tax deduction, one must include a statement of authenticity. Therefore, "for tax purposes, such an appraisal is de facto a representation of authenticity".[21]

Although in that country a professional expert, when performing services for a client, "has the duty to have that degree of learning and skill ordinarily possessed by reputable [members of the profession], practicing in the same or a similar locality and under similar circumstances",[22] appraising personal property—works of art included—in USA is unregulated. That is, the profession is mostly self-regulated.

In the 1980s, the Appraisal Foundation, a non-profit organization was established and it oversees ever since the publication of the Uniform Standards of Professional Appraisal Practice (USPAP). These Standards are only useful guidelines, they are not legally binding.

There are fundamental differences in burden of proof concepts among EU and non-EU jurisdictions.

Under Swiss civil law, the factual question whether a work of art is an authentic work or not must be proven to a "predominant degree of probability" (*überwiegende Wahrscheinlichkeit*). This degree of probability must be established according to the experiences of life; and the accuracy of this material fact must be proven through objective factors.

8.6.1 Corporations as Art Collectors—The Paradigm of Spain

Trying to define the new Spanish cultural landscape, it is absolutely necessary to refer to another factor in the milieu of art collections. A new form of collecting is

[20] Prowda 2013, p. 203.

[21] Prowda 2013, p. 204.

[22] Levy 1991, p. 600.

being observed, especially during the recent decades, having a private nature but acting with a deliberate public projection, as it is pointed out. And this is the corporate collecting.[23]

During the last decades of the 20th century, in a way following the increase of the institutions dedicated to the contemporary art, some enterprises and foundations started creating their own art collections or giving a new dimension to the art collections that they already had created.

These corporate art collections, it is argued, turned the art market more dynamic by founding important galleries dedicated to the national and international contemporary art, while these galleries played an important role in the emergency of new private collectors.

In most cases, these art collections had as their principal reason of being created the corporate image or investment, at the same time though there was a renewed vision of the sponsorship's concept. Corporate collecting in Spain was influenced by what had happened and still happens in other countries but it might also be considered as following a historic line, since in the past too, corporations were sponsoring art.[24]

8.6.2 Corporations as Art Sponsors

As it is stated, "sponsorship is increasingly an important source of income for most collecting institutions".[25] Many art exhibitions can only take place if and when are sponsored by companies, corporations. These companies are sponsoring such events mostly because they have a specific corporate objective to achieve and rarely because of some sort of philanthropy.

Some of the reasons for which the companies are getting involved in art/culture sponsorships are:

- The relationships that are developed between the persons behind the company and the persons associated with the collection, exhibition or project and consequently the personal and corporate profits that will most probably follow.
- The establishment of an image, of a profile in the marketplace.
- The company's image definition and brand development by using the cultural/artistic institution's image.
- The company's image improvement in the community.
- The association with an organization which has a public reputation for excellence.

---

[23] Jiménez-Blanco 2013, p. 91.

[24] Jiménez-Blanco 2013, p. 92.

[25] Simpson 2008.

- The opportunities for networking, for ensuring social access to the usually powerful social circle of persons constituting boards and patrons of collecting organizations, as well as for improving staff or client relations.[26]

In Spain, the tax treatment of the acquisition, maintenance and alienation of cultural objects is dispersed in various laws: Law of Spanish Historic Patrimony, Law 49/2002, on the fiscal regime of the entities without lucrative aim and of the fiscal incentives of the sponsorship, legislation regulating each tax, laws of the autonomous provinces, etc.

A tax deduction of 15 % is foreseen for whichever investment or spending for:

(a) The acquisition of artworks belonging to the Spanish Historic Patrimony that have a cultural interest for the State, are created abroad and reintegrated in the country, on the condition that they have been declared as being of cultural interest or that they have been included in the General Inventory in a time limit of 1 year following their reintegration, and that they remain in Spanish territory and as property of their possessor for a period of at least 4 years.
(b) The conservation, reparation, restoration, diffusion and exhibition of objects that have been declared as being of cultural interest, on the condition that they meet the prerequisites established by the Law of Spanish Historic Patrimony, especially regarding the obligations of public access and exhibition.
(c) The restoration and maintenance of the buildings, of immovables and of goods in Spain that are protected under the Spanish legislation or that would have been declared Patrimony of the Humanity by UNESCO.[27]

According to the Article 1 of the Law 49/2002, sponsorship is the private participation in the realization of activities of general interest ("A efectos de esta Ley, se entiende por mecenazgo la participación privada en la realización de actividades de interés general").

Article 9 of the Constitution guarantees the participation of all citizens in the political, economic, cultural and social life of the State. According to para 2 of the same article, the public authorities have to facilitate this participation.[28]

The Law 49/2002 creates a special tax regime for the non-profit entities, taking into consideration the social function as well as the activities and characteristics of the institutions that would be included in this category. According to a well-founded opinion, these entities receive a privileged tax treatment because they complement or even substitute the public authorities in certain sectors that otherwise should or could be covered by them, but for which there are insufficient

[26] Simpson 2008.

[27] Sobre el estatuto jurídico tributario del coleccionista en España y posibles medidas que contribuyan a su promoción, Informe de la Fundación Arte y Mecenazgo, Barcelona 2014, pp. 15–16. http://fundacionarteymecenazgo.org/wp-content/uploads/2014/08/Informe-estatuto-jur—dico-tributario-del-coleccionista-2014.pdf.

[28] Beneyto Berenguer 2012, pp. 317–318.

resources or there are not at all.[29] Thus, these entities alleviate the State from the burden of providing certain services, something that evidently leads to a saving of public spending.[30]

Among the entities that may be beneficiary of a sponsorship, are the ecclesiastical entities too (Articles 16 and 17 of the Law 49/2002).

In Italy, Article 121 of the Codice dei Beni Culturali e Paesaggisti regulates a specific form of collaboration and sponsoring, with the aim of cultural goods' valorization. This collaboration is being realized by stipulating protocols of intention (*protocolli di intesa*) between the Ministry of Culture or the Regions and other public entities, on the one side, and bank foundations on the other side.[31]

There are bank foundations as well as groups of industry companies which have an interest generally in culture and particularly in museum activities. Trying to handle the issue of the role of these bank foundations in the museums' sector, a study shows the details of this relation and the problems that are created.[32]

A first point is of juridical nature and distinguishes the bank foundations from other private subjects that could have an interest in museum activities. It is an issue that has caused doubts to the juridical theory and the jurisprudence/case-law. According to the Article 1 of the law decree n. 153/1999, one of the "settori ammessi" (admitted sectors) to which the foundations may direct their activity, is the one with the title "Arte, Attivita e Beni Culturali" (Arts, Activities and Cultural Objects) and it is pointed out that the foundations have to direct their own activity exclusively to these admitted sectors.

The Constitutional Court, in its decisions n. 300 and 301, of 24 September 2003, has affirmed that the legislative provisions on the admitted sectors are not in contrast with the constitutional text, since they are referring to all the possible activities and characteristics of the foundations and therefore cannot be considered as contrary to the managerial and statutory autonomy of such entities, which, like every legal person of private law, have to be characterized by "uno scopo" (one aim) that ascertains their activity (Articles 16 and 27 of the Italian Civil Code).

A second point is one of tradition. The bank foundations, since their first appearance in the Italian legal system have been occupied with art. This fact is also statistically proved.[33]

A third point is of macroeconomic nature and refers to factors that are partly contingent and partly structural of the Italian economic system.

---

[29] Pedreira Menéndez 2003, p. 58.

[30] The Dirección General de Tributos, on 10.2.1997 affirmed that: "las entidades sin ánimo de lucro tienen como característica principal y diferenciadora de otras entidades jurídicas que destinan los rendimientos obtenidos en sus distintas actividades a la realización de sus fines sociales, lo cual les faculta para disfrutar de un régimen fiscal ventajoso".

[31] Favretto 2007, p. 125.

[32] Pisaneschi and Perini 2010, p. 35.

[33] Pisaneschi and Perini 2010, pp. 36–37.

After the clarifications obtained by the decisions n. 300 and 301 of the Corte Costituzionale, in 2003, the bank foundations have diversified their "presence fronts" and have proceeded to concrete and new alliances with local entities.

On 19.12.2012, the "Technical norms and guidelines in the matter of sponsorship of cultural goods and of analogous or related cases" (*Norme techniche e line guida in material di sponsorizzazioni di beni culturali e di fattispecie analoghe o collegate*) have been approved by ministerial decree of the Ministry for the cultural goods and activities (*Ministero per I beni e le attivita culturali*).[34]

The discussion, here again, is heated.[35] According to one opinion, the fact that the public funds' extreme scarcity is almost chronic imposes an intense and diversified research for alternative funds in the frame of a public–private collaboration.[36] According to another opinion, this collaboration "has often been invoked but in reality it has only been actuated in the form of concession of services and without renouncing to the public parachute", with the result that private persons have gains and the public sector has damages.[37]

In Switzerland, the net assets—that might include an art collection—are liable to tax property. They are estimated at fair value.[38]

In comparison with the other countries of the world, the taxes in Switzerland are low. Tax deductions are foreseen for the case of donations to tax free foundations which manage museums, to 20 % of the net income (Article 33a Bundesgesetz über die direkte Bundessteuer).[39]

In Australia, there are sources of information for both directions: on the one hand, about potential sponsors available to arts/cultural organizations and on the other hand, about arts organizations (seeking sponsorship) to potential sponsors. About the latter, it is the Australia Foundation for Culture and the Humanities the one that has produced "The Cultural Products Menu".[40]

The sponsorship contracts are negotiated and drafted with care. They really are complex and this is due to their importance and to the monetary value of the sponsorships.

In USA, corporate foundations—there are more than 2,000—give generously to the arts. As it is stated, most major museum exhibitions are sponsored by corporate foundations. "Non-profit art and cultural organizations depend on private foundations including corporate foundations for between a quarter and a half of their operating budgets".[41]

---

[34] Chieppa 2013; Crismani 2013.

[35] Mastragostino 2010; Fidone 2012.

[36] Musso 2013.

[37] Casciu 2013.

[38] Jung 2012, p. 16.

[39] Fischer, p. 64.

[40] http://www.afch.org.au.

[41] Telesetsky 2010.

According to most state and local laws, nonprofit institutions—as the art museums are—are exempted from income, property, and sales taxation. They are also exempt from federal income tax.

It is argued that this exemption does not mean that tax rules have no effect on museums, on the contrary. According to this opinion, the various tax instruments affect art museums indirectly, by changing the incentives of individuals and corporations to make donations of art, by changing the relative cost of raising capital for museum projects, and by changing the incentives of museums to make passive investments in securities rather than active investments in unrelated business.[42]

Obviously, this is a clearly investment-oriented treatment of art, usual perhaps in USA and some other countries of similar economic and political structure, not acceptable though in other countries of different politico-economic culture.

Following the above line of thought (and fact), it is pointed out that for art museums in USA, a very important form of donation is an artwork that has appreciated in value since the time of acquisition by the donor.[43]

In common law countries sponsorship by private persons too constitutes a very important axis of culture financing. In most of the other—if not all—countries, no special tax regime is foreseen, as is the case for the corporations.[44] This difference of treatment, especially the fact that the percentage of tax deduction is inferior for the natural persons than that for the juridical persons, is a reason of complaining by both prospective sponsors and jurists of those countries, especially during the recent years.[45]

References

Aguilar Rubio M, Ciarcia AR (2005) Régimen tributario comparado del mecenazgo en España e Italia. Revista de Estudios Cooperativos (REVESCO) 86:7–21. www.redalyc.org/pdf/367/36708600

Barraca de Ramos P (2008) El mercado de arte y la política de adquisición de colecciones públicas. In: Prado Román C, Vico Belmonte A (coord) La inversión en bienes de colección. Universidad Rey Juan Carlos, Madrid, pp 61–78

Beneyto Berenguer R (2012) Régimen tributario de los bienes culturales de titularidad ecclesiástica. In: Vega Gutiérrez AM, Martín Garcia M del Mar, Rodríguez Blanco M, Vázquez García-Peñuela JM (coords) Protección del Patrimonio Cultural de Interés Religioso. Actas del V Simposio Internacional de Derecho Concordatario, Logroño, 19–21 de octubre de 2011. Editorial Comares, Granada, pp 245–347

Casciu S (2013) Il tema delle sponsorizzazioni/erogazioni liberali visto dalla parte delle Soprintendenze: difficolta, equivoci, burocrazia, mentalita. Aedon no 2. http://www.aedon.mulino.it/archivio/2013/2/casciu.htm

[42] Fullerton 1991, p. 195.

[43] Fullerton 1991, p. 195.

[44] Aguilar Rubio and Ciarcia 2005, pp. 20–21.

[45] Zanetti 2001.

Cerviño M (2011) Nuevo coleccionismo de arte argentino contemporáneo. El caso de Gustavo Bruzzone. Arte y Sociedad. Rev Invest. www.eumad.net/rev/ays/0/mc.html

Chieppa R (2013) Il nuovo regime delle erogazioni liberali e delle sponsorizzazioni: il settore dei beni culturali e l'intervento delle fondazioni. Aedon no 2. http://www.aedon.mulino.it/archivio/2013/2/chieppa.htm

Crismani A (2013) I musei tra l'immaginario colletivo e la realta giuridica e gestionale. Aedon no 3. http://www.aedon.mulino.it/archivio/2013/3/crismani.htm

Favretto S (2007) Il diritto a braccetto con l'arte. Opportunita e tutele giuridiche nei beni culturali e paesaggistici, nel mercato delle opera d'arte. Edizioni Falsopiano, Alessandria

Fidone G (2012) Il ruolo dei privati nella valorizzazione dei beni culturali: dalle sponsorizzazioni alle forme di gestione. Aedon nos 1–2. http://www.aedon.mulino.it/archivio/2012/1_2/fidone.htm

Fischer K Schweiz – Ein Paradies für Sammler? Art Value 6:64–70. www.fischerauktionen.ch/UserData/Download_45813_00.pdf

Frey BS (2009) Cultural economics. CESifo DICE Rep 7(1):20–25

Frey BS, Meier S (2002) Museums between private and public. The case of the Beyeler Museum in Basle. Working paper no 116, Institute for Empirical Research in Economics, University of Zurich. http://ssrn.com/abstract=316698

Fullerton D (1991) Tax Policy toward art museums. In: Feldstein M (ed) The economics of art museums. The University of Chicago Press, Chicago, pp 195–236. http://www.nber.org/chapters/c11643

Hutter M, Frey BS (2010) On the influence of cultural value on economic value. Rev Econ Polit 120:35–46

Jay H (2009) A picture imperfect: the rights of art consignor-collectors when their art dealer files for bankruptcy. Duke Law J 58:1859–1893

Jiménez-Blanco MD (2013) El coleccionismo de arte en España. Una aproximación desde su historia y su contexto. Fundación Arte y Mecenazgo, Barcelona. www.fudacionarteymecenazgo.org/wp-content/uploads/2014/10/el-coleccionismo-de-arte-en-espa—a.pdf

Jung MR (2012) Der Kunstsammler im Schweizer Steuergefüge. In: Mosimann P, Schönenberger B (hrsg) Kunst & Recht/Art & Law. Stämpfli Verlag, Bern, pp 15–38

Levy SM (1991) Liability of the art expert for professional malpractice. Wis Law Rev 595

Mastragostino F (2010) Sponsorizzazioni e pubbliche amministrazioni; caratteri generali e fattori di specialita. Aedon no 1. http://www.aedon.mulino.it/archivio/2010/1/mastragostino.htm

McAndrew C (2012) El Mercado Español del Arte en 2012. Fundación Arte y Mecenazgo, Barcelona

Musso A (2013) La sponsorizzazione come contratto commerciale. Aedon no 2. http://www.aedon.mulino.it/archivio/2013/2/musso.htm

Pedreira Menéndez J (2003) El régimen fiscal del sector no lucrativo y del mecenazgo. Thomson-Aranzadi, Pamplona

Pérez-Bustamante Yábar D (2008) Fundaciones y coleccionismo: experiencias y tendencias. In: Prado Román C, Vico Belmonte A (coord) La inversión en bienes de colección. Universidad Rey Juan Carlos, Madrid, pp 190–211

Pisaneschi A, Perini M (2010) Fondazioni e musei. Il ruolo delle fondazioni bancarie: dal finanziamento alla gestione. In: Morbidelli G, Cerrina Feroni G (a cura di) I musei. Discipline, gestioni, prospettive. G. Giappichelli Editore, Torino pp 35–58

Prowda JB (2013) Visual arts and the law. A handbook for professionals. Lund Humphries in association with Sotheby's Institute of Art, Farnham, Burlington–London, New York

Rosett RN (1991) Art museums in the United States: a financial portrait. In: Feldstein M (ed) The economics of art museums. The University of Chicago Press, Chicago, pp 129–178. http://www.nber.org/chapters/c11641

Simpson S (2008) Collections law. Legal issues for Australian archives, galleries, libraries and museums (chapter 30. Sponsorship). http://www.collectionslaw.com.au

Steiner L, Frey BS, Resch M (2013) Home is where your art is: the home bias of art collectors. Working paper no 135, University of Zurich, Department of Economics. www.zora.uzh.ch/85620/1/econwp135.pdf

Steinkamp JG (1994) Fair market value, blockage, and the valuation of art. Denver Univ Law Rev 71:335–425

Telesetsky A (2010) Corporate Foundations and US Cultural Heritage: role of US corporate in protecting and promoting the built Cultural Heritage sector. Aedon no 1. http://www.aedon.mulino.it/archivio/2010/1/telesetsky.htm

Zanetti L (2001) Gli strumenti di sostegno alla cultura tra pubblico e private. Aedon no 2. www.aedon.mulino.it/archivio/2001/2/zanetti.htm

Chapter 9
Museums and Collectors and the Illicit Trade of Art/Cultural Objects

9.1 General Comments

Unfortunately the trade in looted art and antiquities is one of the most prolific illicit trades in the world. Obviously, this trade is a "demand-driven crime", it takes place because it is already known by the looters that there are buyers waiting for these objects.[1] Artifacts are looted almost regularly from the so-called "source countries",[2] such as Italy, Greece, Iraq, India, China, Peru, Egypt, and others too.[3]

Circulating rumors and charges for art theft[4] have led to the increase of prosecutions against private galleries/dealers and collectors but also against museums,[5] since they are considered as playing a significant role in the black market art network.

Recently it was estimated that the international market for cultural objects is about $60 billion. The value of the market for illegally acquired objects is about $billion—low because this sort of crime is under-reported.[6]

It is generally known that [some] museums have a big share of responsibility for all these purchases of looted cultural objects in the past, either for having a conscientiously unethical behavior or for not searching enough whether the cultural objects they had purchased had good provenance.

---

[1] Amineddoleh 2013, p. 228.

[2] It was John H. Merryman who first used these two "terms", "market nations" and "source nations", as far as the antiquities are concerned, see Merryman 1986, p. 832.

[3] Bogdanos 2008, p. 725; Vitale 2009, p. 1835.

[4] According to Kreder and Bauer 2011, p. 882: "Art theft is rampant for a number of reasons: the news headlines of art auctions fetching millions of dollars, the notoriously lax security of art museums, and the low priority of art theft investigations due to the perception that the crime is "victimless".

[5] Resulting in "bad publicity and immense financial expense" for the museums, see Dubin 2010, p. 132.

[6] Amineddoleh 2013, p. 235.

E. Moustaira, *Art Collections, Private and Public: A Comparative Legal Study*, SpringerBriefs in Law, DOI 10.1007/978-3-319-15802-0_9

Several U.S. museums and U.S. university museums had done it in the past—The Metropolitan Museum of New York,[7] the Cleveland Museum of Art, the John P. Getty Museum, the Museum of Fine Arts in Boston, the Princeton University Art Museum, etc.

These last years, one observes a wave of actions being filed before the U.S. and other countries' courts, by national governments demanding the restitution of these objects.[8] It is estimated that the fear of actions that could be filed by source countries would reduce the incentive for theft of art objects.

Also new claims will certainly continue to arise as thefts of artworks from museums, galleries, offices, homes, occur all over the world and too often, unfortunately.[9]

The results are not always so clear in the "market countries", as the USA for example, and there is not much case law. Although many are the voices in favor of prosecuting and increasing the criminal penalties[10] for the art theft network,[11] in order to deter such thefts, other jurists are reluctant to do that, arguing that art theft is a victimless crime—a completely inaccurate observation, since theft of cultural objects is linked to organized crime syndicates.

9.2 Export Prohibitions or Restrictions—Limited or Not

This is one of the most important issues concerning cultural objects, in which many opposite tendencies are met: on the one hand protection of art objects considered as formative elements of national identities and on the other hand protection of the proprietary rights (if and when such rights are recognized to private persons).

Given the fact that during the previous centuries—especially the 18th and 19th—many cultural objects were removed from their countries of origin, without any care about the legality of these acts, most of the countries—victims enacted legislation protecting their own treasures, their own cultural property, their own cultural heritage. Among the protective measures were and are export prohibition or export restrictions.

Things were not always clear, as far as museum collections were concerned. At the beginning of the 20th century, when the "landscape" of cultural objects' protection was not strictly designed in various national laws, there were even some very strange "cases" of persons who led a sort of double life: on the one hand they

[7] Thomas Hoving, the former director of the Metropolitan Museum, openly acknowledged—in a book he wrote, in 1993—that museums had a very significant role in the purchase of looted cultural objects. It is cited by Amineddoleh 2013, p. 235.

[8] Hoffman 2010, pp. 667–668.

[9] Hilaire and Davis 2010, p. 37.

[10] Kreder 2005, p. 1199.

[11] Scott Dutcher 2006, p. 1295; Ulph 2011, p. 39.

were trying to conserve artworks of their country, as important items of national artistic collections, and on the other hand they were involved in the art market selling abroad such artworks, either with the aim of acquiring the money that would be needed for their "first life" or in order to make their national artworks known abroad.[12]

Things have changed. The circulation of cultural objects has reached "withering heights". Some people, some countries are—not always licitly—advantaged, while others are considering themselves unprotected from the means that are used to remove cultural objects from their "cradle". Therefore, strict approaches are adopted, considered as self-evidence, especially in the second case.

These strict approaches may vary, especially in the case of undiscovered cultural objects. Thus, several countries declare all undiscovered antiquities state property, while others restrict the export.

The scope of export prohibitions or restrictions of cultural objects in general, varies substantially in the countries of the world.[13] Some national laws are very lenient and some are moderately restrictive, while others are highly restrictive. Especially the "art-rich" countries, the "source nations" are extensively restrictive.[14]

In USA, the law does not contain any provision that specifically prohibits the export of cultural objects. The consequence is that cultural objects may be freely exported unless they have been acquired "in violation of federal or state laws governing the status and disposition of cultural and other resources on public or Native American land as well as on private land to some extent".[15]

In Switzerland, in the past there were no export restrictions at the federal level. After 1.6.2005, date of entry into force of the Federal Act on the International Transfer of Cultural Property, it is expressly required to declare cultural property at the border. According to the Article 25 para 1 of the above Act, the declaration must contain the type of cultural object and its place of origin.[16]

In Greece, the Law 3028/2002, actually in force, regulates in a very detailed way the export of cultural objects.[17]

---

[12] Such is the case of Marqués de Vega-Inclán, according to Kagan 2013, pp. 199–200. At about 1904, on the one hand he had dreams such as planning a new museum in Toledo, dedicated to the works of El Greco, and on the other hand he was directly or indirectly implicated in the sale of paintings (probably 20 of them…) of the same painter to buyers abroad. As Kagan mentions, Marqués de Vega-Inclán was so much enthusiastic about this project of making a new museum in Toledo, that a friend of his, Aureliano Beruete y Moret, art historian, art critic, and director of the Museo del Prado in 1918 (and having the same attitude with Marqués de Vega-Inclán, as far as selling works of Spanish painters abroad is concerned) was thinking that Marqués de Vega-Inclán was suffering from an illness that he was describing as "theotocapulifila manía"!.

[13] See Paterson and Renold 2014, pp. 572–573: "Overall, however, amongst developed countries there is a patchwork of national cultural property export controls that often bear little resemblance to one another, in wording or implementation".

[14] Fincham 2008, p. 349.

[15] Nafziger 2014a, p. 509.

[16] Renold and Schönenberger 2014, pp. 409, 414.

[17] Moustaira 2014, pp. 183–187.

According to Article 34 of this Law and as a general rule, the export of monuments from the Hellenic territory is prohibited, with specific exceptions (§ 1). Accordingly, the export of monuments is allowed, following the issuance of a permit, only in case these monuments are not of particular importance for the cultural heritage of the country and the integrity of important collections is not wounded. A permit of export may be issued specifically for monuments of the last 100 years if their retention in the country is not considered to be necessary (§§ 2&3).

The export of monuments that belong to and possessed by the State may be permitted if the conditions of Article 25 are met. This article refers to the loan and exchange of movable monuments that belong to the State.

By decision of the Minister of Culture, following a report of the pertinent Service and a legal opinion of the pertinent Council, published movable monuments that belong to and are possessed by the State may, in exceptional circumstances, be loaned to museums or educational organizations for exhibitions or pedagogic purposes. Loans to museums may take place in terms of reciprocity.[18]

The Law 3028/2002, in this chapter, also foresees criminal sanctions for the illicit export and import of cultural objects.[19]

It is rightly argued that, in comparison with other source countries, Greece has not an excessively restrictive legal regime as far as the export of cultural goods, especially antiquities, is concerned.[20]

In United Kingdom, the Export of Objects of Cultural Interest (Control) Order 2003 provides in its Article 2 that *all* objects of cultural interest are prohibited from being exported to any destination except under the authority of a written licence granted by the Secretary of State, and in accordance with all the conditions attached to the licence.[21]

In the case of cultural objects considered as of national importance, a special regime applies since 1953. And the question of whether a cultural object is of national importance is being answered by applying the Waverley Criteria—thus called, following the report, in 1952, of the committee under the chairmanship of Viscount Waverley.[22]

According to that system, cultural objects must be assessed against the following tree criteria:

"Waverley one": Is the object so closely connected with our history or national life that its departure would be a misfortune?

"Waverley two": Is it of outstanding aesthetic importance?

---

18 For more details about the Greek law, see Moustaira 2014, pp. 183–186.

19 Moustaira 2014, pp. 186–187.

20 Voudouri 2010, p. 557.

21 Chamberlain and Hausler 2014, p. 469.

22 Wang 2008, p. 227.

"Waverley three": Is it of outstanding significance for the study of some particular branch of art, learning or history?".[23]

As it is stated, many Commonwealth countries have adopted some version of the "Waverley Criteria". In some of these countries, though, there are significant differences in practice. For example, in New Zealand, a country that has adopted the Waverley Criteria, permissions to export Maori artifacts are rarely granted, independently of whether these artifacts are "significant" or not.[24]

In Canada, controls on the export of cultural objects are established by the Cultural Property Export and Import Act (CPEIA) which, as it is pointed out, was entered into force on 6.9.1977, just before Canada became party to the 1970 UNESCO Convention on the Means of Prohibiting and Preventing the Illicit Import, Export and Transfer of Ownership of Cultural Property as well as the 1954 UNESCO Convention for the Protection of Cultural Property in the Event of Armed Conflict and its protocols of 1954 and 1999.[25] Thus the Act also implements the 1970 Convention[26] into Canadian domestic law.

The CPEIA imposes export controls on cultural property originating both in Canada and elsewhere, just like UK law does.[27]

The two main reasons for the inclusion of non-Canadian objects in this control scheme are connected, as stated, with the fact that cultural objects which have been in Canada for less than 35 years are exempted from the CPEIA: (a) this period, of 35 years, is the average span of collecting by individuals, therefore they can, during this period, freely import and export cultural objects; (b) non-Canadian objects are considered as becoming "Canadian" after having been in the country for more than 35 years.[28]

Some scholars believe that the "legal environment affects the behavior of buyers in import countries, who are most affected by source countries' export-related legal activities".[29] They argue that the threat of criminal or civil prosecution because of acquiring an object the export of which was prohibited or restricted in its country of origin, as well as the threat of its seizure, makes buyers reluctant to purchase cultural objects that would subject them to legal liability. It is not always so, though.

---

[23] Chamberlain and Hausler 2014, p. 472.

[24] Davies and Myburgh 2008, p. 321.

[25] See infra, 9.3.

[26] Paterson 2014, p. 74.

[27] See Paterson 2014, p. 75, stating that the Canadian Act "also relied on French experience insofar as it provided for a decentralized system of administration".

[28] Clark 1982–1983, p. 775.

[29] Stoll 2012, p. 66.

9.3 International Conventions, European Union Rules and Trade of Cultural Objects

On an international level, the trade of cultural objects is regulated by the UNESCO Convention of 1970 on the Means of Prohibiting and Preventing the Illicit Import, Export and Transfer of Ownership of Cultural Property[30] and the UNIDROIT Convention of 1995 on Stolen or Illegally Exported Cultural Objects.[31] As it is stated, these two conventions offer the structure necessary for the cooperation between countries in order to fight the illicit trade of cultural objects.[32]

Both International Conventions have to be ratified and received in the national laws of the countries in order to be applicable to them.

In the European Union countries, there are the Council Regulation (EC) No 116/2009 on the export of cultural goods, and the Directive 2014/60/EU on the return of cultural objects unlawfully removed from the territory of a Member State and amending Regulation (EU) No 1024/2012 (the Directive 93/7, as amended, is repealed with effect from 15 December 2015).

UNESCO Convention 1970 has been ratified by 120 countries.[33] USA ratified it in 1983, with the Cultural Property Implementation Act, 19 U.S.C. §§ 2601. UNIDROIT Convention 1995 has been ratified by 36 countries[34]—not by USA.

The UK is a party to the 1970 UNESCO Convention but it made several reservations when it accepted it (in 2002). For the implementation of the Convention, UK has enacted the DEALING in Cultural Objects (Offences) Act 2003.[35]

UK has lists of cultural property for the Open General Export Licence, the Open Individual Export Licences and the Individual Licences. EU also has categories of cultural property. UK considered that the list of various categories of cultural property that the 1970 UNESCO Convention contains, differs from both UK Categories and EU categories, therefore she accepted it by making those reservations.[36]

UK is not a party to the 1995 UNIDROIT Convention. According to the conclusions of the Secretary of State for Culture, Media and Sport, certain UNIDROIT

---

[30] See Nafziger 2014b, p. 211, on the fact that it was Mexico, "that, along with Peru, initiated specific legal efforts to combat illegal trafficking". These efforts led to the 1970 UNESCO Convention.

[31] Estrella Faria 2014, p. 19.

[32] See Kaye 2014, p. 209: "Through the 1970 UNESCO Convention and the 1995 UNIDROIT Convention, the international community has taken important steps to try to rationalize the varied international response to stolen cultural property, foster widespread international enforcement of national ownership laws and, albeit gingerly at first, sanction the enforcement by one nation of another nation's export laws in a way that adequately reflects the concerns of source and market countries".

[33] http://portal.unesco.org/la/convention.asp?KO=13039&language=E.

[34] www.unidroit.org/status-cp.

[35] Chamberlain and Hausler 2014, pp. 461–462.

[36] See http://portal.unesco.org/en/ev.php-URL_ID=13039&URL_DO=D)_TOPIC&URL_SECTION=201.htm#RESERVES.

Convention's rules were in conflict with UK's domestic law, in particular those concerning the limitations periods and personal property.[37]

The fact that USA has ratified the UNESCO Convention is very important since, as it has already been mentioned, it is one of the biggest art markets due to the demand for many and various cultural objects both by private collectors and museums.

At first, the participants to the art market were absolutely negative to the perspective of ratification by USA of the UNESCO Convention, considering it as a limitation of the international trade of cultural objects.[38] Nevertheless, the Archaeological Institute of America persuaded the U.S. Congress to ratify the Convention as a diplomatic act and at the same time act of moral leadership. That way, the collaboration between archaeologists of USA and of countries of origin would be facilitated.[39]

The Cultural Property Implementation Act of 1983 introduced in USA a mechanism which prohibits the import of cultural objects[40] that are documented in national catalogues, if these catalogues are contained in the provisions of bilateral agreements (Memoranda) between USA and the countries of origin, members of the UNESCO Convention.[41]

Until now, USA have signed such bilateral agreements with seventeen countries: Belize, Bolivia, Bulgaria, Cambodia, Canada, China, Colombia, Cyprus, El Salvador, Greece, Guatemala, Honduras, Iraq, Italy, Mali, Nicaragua, Peru.[42]

In European countries, there is a great variety of the modes of incorporation of the 1970 UNESCO Convention in their internal law. Furthermore, there are several difficulties mainly regarding the realization of the aims of the Convention, either because the solutions chosen by the States are different between each other and consequently the protection offered is not on the same level or because certain rules, deemed necessary by the Convention, have not been enacted.[43]

---

[37] Chamberlain and Hausler 2014, p. 462.

[38] Most jurists in USA oppose in generally to a "blank check rule", according to which USA would be expected to enforce foreign export restrictions, see Merryman 2001, p. 51. However, the *McClain* doctrine incorporates some foreign law into title issues. Under this doctrine, dealing in antiquities that have been excavated in violation of a foreign statute can result in criminal sanctions in USA, even when U.S. import regulations have not been violated, see Goldberg 2006, p. 1031.

[39] Beltrametti 2013. She points out that the UNESCO Convention's entry into force in USA was not at all of interest of the country, for two major reasons: First, the U.S. cultural objects are scarce and not of particular interest to the international market, therefore they did not really need the guaranteed by the UNESCO Convention protection. Second, the introduction of a regulation that would make more difficult the work of the traders and of curators, would reduce the trade of cultural objects and, consequently, the world prestige of important U.S. collections.

[40] The illicit import in USA has both civil [19 U.S.C. § 2609 (2012)] and criminal [National Stole Property Act, 18 U.S.C. §§ 2314-15 (2012)] consequences.

[41] 19 U.S.C. § 2602(a)(2)(A),(B) (2012).

[42] http://exchanges.state.gov/heritage.culprop/listactions.html (Nov. 17, 2014).

[43] Cornu 2014, p. 83.

"It is apparent that the 1970 Convention was never a perfect instrument. Nor has it been uniformly implemented by States Parties. How can we make it more effective?", is being asked. It does not seem appropriate or advisable to reform the Convention or amend some of its provisions. There are new principles of international law, that even being soft law, as initiatives can be very effective in contributing to the combatting of illicit trade of cultural objects.[44]

Such initiatives are, for example, the I.L.A. Principles for Cooperation in the Mutual Protection and Transfer of Cultural Material, adopted in 2006, as well as the UNESCO's 2012 Model Provisions on State Ownership of Undiscovered Cultural Objects.[45]

Of course "there is still much to be done to ensure support for the protection of cultural heritage from the blights of theft, clandestine excavation and smuggling".[46]

9.4 Italy v. Marion True and Robert Hecht

In 2005, Marion True, a curator of antiquities at the J. Paul Getty Museum in Los Angeles, was charged, by Italian prosecutors, with criminal association and receipt of stolen property in connection with antiquities believed to have been illegally excavated in Italy and smuggled out of the country.

The charge referred to her activities during a time period from the mid-1980s through to 1998. She was alleged to have knowingly obtained more than 40 archaeological objects illegally excavated by *tombarolli* or stolen in Italy. It was the first time that an American museum official was prosecuted abroad for alleged art crime.[47]

Since the 90s, the Carabinieri[48] had started a rigid research about how they would succeed the repatriation of objects illegally exported from the Italian territory. In 1995, they raided a storage room in the Geneva Freeport in Switzerland, that belonged to a notorious dealer of looted antiquities, Giacomo Medici and that was filled with illicitly acquired artifacts as well as documents and photographs. Marion True had dealt with Medici and Robert Hecht, his business partner.[49]

In 1997, Giacomo Medici was arrested and condemned by the Tribunal of Rome to imprisonment of 10 years and to 10 million euros for having illegally exported and sold, during many years, thousands of Italian artworks. The evidence acquired during this proceeding has permitted the procurators in Rome, to incriminate Marion True and Robert Hecht.[50]

---

[44] Nafziger 2014a, b, p. 228.

[45] Frigo 2011, p. 1024.

[46] Prott 2014, p. 294.

[47] Amineddoleh 2013, p. 240.

[48] "Comando dei Carabinieri" which is exclusively occupied with the national cultural patrimony's care.

[49] Founder of the department store chain that bears his surname; see also about the case, Scott 2008, pp. 806–810.

[50] Beltrametti 2013.

In October 2010, both cases—against Marion True and Robert Hecht—ended because of expiration of the statute of limitations. Nevertheless, the impact of this case was big and it is hoped that it has managed to pressure international collectors and museums to verify the origin of the artifacts they are buying.[51]

It is argued that one method for preventing international looting of art objects, for preservation of art,[52] is for museums or collectors to lend them to other museums and collectors. That is what Italy has started to do during the last 10 years.

For example, in 2006, following a proposal of the Italian Ministry of Culture to the Metropolitan Museum of New York, it was agreed between them such a loan: In exchange for the return of 21 looted Italian antiquities—the most important of which was Euphronios Krater—the Italian Government agreed to lend the Metropolitan Museum comparable artifacts for 4 years. Furthermore, the Metropolitan Museum received permission to sponsor excavations in Italy and take finds to USA.

Not every country acquiesces to such a solution though, since it does not really solve the problem of artworks ownership, among its other problems and non-clarified issues.[53]

9.5 Immunity of Collections from Suit or Seizure

Loan of cultural objects to institutions in other states sometimes causes fear to the prospective lenders—be it states or private persons—that they could be seized by third-party claimants who would take advantage of the change in jurisdiction.[54]

Claims by third parties may arise in three cases: (a) a government, a company or an individual may claim to be the owner of a cultural object, file a suit asking to have that ownership recognized, and seek to take possession of the object; (b) a claimant may ask for the seizure of a cultural object—treated as an asset—in order to enforce a judgment issued against the owner; (c) the cultural object may be seized as part of a criminal investigation.[55]

Immunity from seizure or suit statutes' aim is to prevent either the seizure of borrowed cultural objects that might have been ordered by a court or other legally imposed restraint on their physical movement or a suit against them.

It is pointed out that concerns about seizure of borrowed cultural objects first arose in the early 1960s when U.S. museums thought about borrowing artworks from the Soviet Union. Soviet Union, worried that claims might be made against

---

[51] See Stoll 2012, p. 91: "For antiquities collectors, museums, and educational institutions, the battle has just begun. Recent victories have emboldened the Italian government, and it continues to launch investigations into American institutions' acquisitions".

[52] Goodwin 2008, pp. 689–691.

[53] Loschelder 2010, p. 705.

[54] See Palmer 2005, p. 950: "Public exhibition exposes cultural objects to widespread scrutiny, alerting potential claimants".

[55] Forrest 2014, p. 144; Getz 2011, pp. 205–209.

these artworks (that had been nationalized after the 1917 revolution) while being in USA, asked for some guarantee that they would be given back to Russia after the agreed time.

In 1965, the [Federal] Immunity from Seizure Act (22 U.S.C. Section 2459) was adopted. It was followed by legislation in four states: New York (Arts and Cultural Affairs Law, Section 12.03), Rhode Island (General Laws, Section 5-62), Texas (Civil Practice and Remedies Code, Section 3-61), and Tennessee (Tennessee Code, Section 28-3-115).

In the following years, more countries adopted such laws.[56] In Canada, five provinces have enacted immunity from seizure laws: Manitoba (Foreign Cultural Objects Immunity from Seizure Act, C.C.S.M. 1987, c. F-140), Québec (Code of Civil Procedure R.S.Q. 1976, c. C-25), Ontario (Foreign Cultural Objects Immunity from Seizure Act, R.S.O. 1990, c. F-23), British Columbia (Law and Equity Act, R. S.B.C. 1996, c. 253), and Alberta (Foreign Cultural Property Immunity Act, R.S.A. 2000, c. F-17).

France enacted such a law in 1994, Germany in 1998 (Gesetz zum Schutz deutschen Kulturgutes gegen Abwanderung, BGB1. I 1955, 501, as amended by Gesetz zur Umsetzung von Richtlinien der Europäischen Gemeinschaften, 26.5.1998), Belgium in 2002, Austria in 2003, Switzerland and Lichtenstein in 2005, Israel and United Kingdom in 2007, Finland, Czech Republic, and Japan in 2011, Hungary in 2012, and Australia in 2013 (Protection of Cultural Objects on Loan Act).

In some of these countries, the relevant legislation provides broad protection to cultural objects lent by foreign countries. This is the case for example of U.S. and of United Kingdom. It is stressed though, that it will be the courts that will determine how far this protection reaches.[57]

The Australian Act, borrowing the scheme followed by U.K. respective legislation,[58] establishes institutional immunity, that is, immunity arises only when cultural objects are imported in the country under an agreement between a lender and a borrowing institution that has been approved by the minister. In many other countries, as it is mentioned, such as Canada, France, Germany and Israel, in order that immunity is granted, a specific request has to be filed which will specify the objects for which immunity is being asked.

Comments on this recent Australian law, point out that "it remains to be seen whether this statute with such a wide immunity will function as intended".[59]

---

[56] All these details about legislations are taken from the articles of Forrest 2014, p. 144 and Getz 2011, p. 203.

[57] Kaye 2010, p. 354.

[58] O'Connell 2009, p. 783.

[59] Forrest 2014, p. 163.

Cultural Heritage Law Committee of the International Law Association completed in 2014 a Draft Convention on Immunity from Suit and Seizure for Cultural Objects Temporarily Abroad for Cultural, Educational or Scientific Purposes. This Draft Convention is intended for eventual adoption by an international or regional organization and ratification of it by states.[60]

References

Amineddoleh L (2013) The role of museums in the trade of black market cultural heritage property. Art Antiq Law 18:227–254

Beltrametti S (2013) Dati e analisi sul traffic illecito dei beni culturali. Aedon no 1. www.aedon.mulino.it/archivio/2013/1/betrametti.htm

Bogdanos M (2008) Thieves of Baghdad: combating global traffic in stolen Iraqi antiquities. Fordham Int Law J 31:725–740

Chamberlain K, Hausler K (2014) United Kingdom. In: Nafziger JAR, Paterson RK (eds) Handbook on the law of cultural heritage and international trade. Edward Elgar, Cheltenham, pp 460–505

Clark IC (1982–1983) The cultural property export and import act of Canada: legislation to encourage national co-operation. New York Univ J Int Law Policy 15:771–787

Cornu M (2014) La mise en œuvre de la Convention UNESCO de 1970 en Europe. In: Sánchez Cordero JA (ed) La Convención de la UNESCO de 1970. Sus nuevos desafíos. Universidad Nacional Autónoma de México, México, pp 79–87

Davies P, Myburgh P (2008) The protected objects act in New Zealand: too little, too late? Int J Cult Property 15:321–345

Dubin R (2010) Museums and self-regulation: assessing the impact of newly promulgated guidelines on the litigation of cultural property. Univ Miami Bus Law Rev 18:101–140

Estrella Faria JA (2014) UNESCO, UNIDROIT y la restitución de bienes culturales. In: Sánchez Cordero JA (ed) La Convención de la UNESCO de 1970. Sus nuevos desafíos. Universidad Nacional Autónoma de México, México, pp 19–33

Fincham D (2008) A coordinated legal and policy approach to undiscovered antiquities: adapting the cultural heritage policy of England and Wales to other nations of origin. Int J Cult Property 15:347–370

Forrest C (2014) Immunity from seizure and suit in Australia: the protection of cultural objects on loan act 2013. Int J Cult Property 21:143–172

Frigo M (2011) Model provisions on state ownership of undiscovered cultural objects: introduction. Unif Law Rev 16:1024–1035

Getz D (2011) The history of Canadian immunity from seizure legislation. Int J Cult Property 18:201–224

Goldberg A (2006) Reaffirming McClain: the national stolen property act and the abiding trade in looted cultural objects. UCLA Law Rev 53:1031–1071

Goodwin PS (2008) Mapping the limits of repatriable cultural heritage: a case study of stolen Flemish art in French museums. Univ PA Law Rev 157:673–705

Hoffman MR (2010) Cultural pragmatism: a new approach to the international movement of antiquities. Iowa Law Rev 95:665–694

Kagan R (2013) El Marqués de Vega-Inclán y el patrimonio artístico español. ¿Protector o expoliador?. In: Socias I, Gkozgkou D (eds) Nuevas contribuciones en torno al mundo del

60 See Summary of ILA's 76th Conference—Washington 2014, April 12, 2014, p. 13.

coleccionismo de arte hispánico en los siglos XIX y XX. Ediciones Trea, Gijón (Asturias), pp 193–215
Kaye LM (2010) Art loans and immunity from seizure in the United States and the United Kingdom. Int J Cult Property 17:335–359
Kaye LM (2014) The fight against the illicit trafficking of cultural property: best practices in the United States of America. In: Sánchez Cordero JA (ed) La Convención de la UNESCO de 1970. Sus nuevos desafíos. Universidad Nacional Autónoma de México, México, pp 175–210
Kreder JA (2005) The choice between civil and criminal remedies in stolen art litigation. Vanderbilt J Transnatl Law 38:1199–1252
Kreder JA, Bauer B (2011) Protecting property rights and unleashing capital in art. Utah Law Rev, pp 881–925
Loschelder M (2010) Die Dauerleihgabe, ein in der Museumspraxis gängiger, rechtlicher aber unscharfer und weitgehend ungeklärter Begriff. Neue Juristische Wochenschrift, pp 705–709
Merryman JH (1986) Two ways of thinking about cultural property. Am J Int Law 80:831–853
Merryman JH (2001) Cultural property, international trade and human rights. Cardozo Arts Entertain Law J 19:51–67
Moustaira EN (2014) Greece. In: Nafziger JAR, Paterson RK (eds) Handbook on the law of cultural heritage and international trade. Edward Elgar, Cheltenham, pp 176–191
Nafziger JAR (2014a) United States. In: Nafziger JAR, Paterson RK (eds) Handbook on the law of cultural heritage and international trade. Edward Elgar, Cheltenham, pp 506–531
Nafziger JAR (2014b) The 1970 UNESCO convention: insights, circumspections, and outlooks. In: Sánchez Cordero JA (ed) La Convención de la UNESCO de 1970. Sus nuevos desafíos. Universidad Nacional Autónoma de México, México, pp 211–228
O'Connell A (2009) The United Kingdom's immunity from seizure legislation. Modern Law Rev 72:783–793
Palmer N (2005) Adrift on a sea of troubles: cross-border art loans and the specter of ulterior title. Vanderbilt J Transnatl Law 38:947–996
Paterson RK (2014) Canada. In: Nafziger JAR, Paterson RK (eds) Handbook on the law of cultural heritage and international trade. Edward Elgar, Cheltenham, pp 74–106
Paterson RK, Renold MA (2014) Foreign culture: export controls on material of foreign origin. In: Nafziger JAR, Paterson RK (eds) Handbook on the law of cultural heritage and international trade. Edward Elgar, Cheltenham, pp 571–588
Prott LV (2014) Philosophies, politics, law and the 1970 UNESCO convention. In: Sánchez Cordero JA (ed) La Convención de la UNESCO de 1970. Sus nuevos desafíos. Universidad Nacional Autónoma de México, México, pp 269–295
Renold MA, Schönenberger B (2014) Switzerland. In: Nafziger JAR, Paterson RK (eds) Handbook on the law of cultural heritage and international trade. Edward Elgar, Cheltenham, pp 408–436
Scott GR (2008) Spoliation, cultural property, and Japan. Univ PA J Int Law 29:803–902
Scott Dutcher J (2006) From the boardroom to the cell block: the justifications for harsher punishment of white-collar and corporate crime. Arizona State Law J 37:1295–1319
St Hilaire R, Davis T (2010) Art and antiquity trafficking news notes. Cult Herit Arts Rev 1(1):37–39. www.lootedart.com/web_images/pdf2/CHAReviewI%20first%20edition%20Spring%202010.pdf
Stoll CS (2012) The effects of judicial decisions and patrimony laws on the price of Italian antiquities. Int J Cult Property 19:65–96
Ulph J (2011) The impact of the criminal law and money laundering measures upon the illicit trade in art and antiquities. Art Antiq Law 16:39–52
Vitale KD (2009) The war on antiquities: United States law and foreign cultural property. Notre Dame Law Rev 84:1835–1875
Voudouri D (2010) Law and the politics of the past: legal protection of cultural heritage in Greece. Int J Cult Property 17:547–568
Wang V (2008) Whose responsibility? The Waverley system past and present. Int J Cult Property 15:227–269

Chapter 10
Conclusions: The Ethics of Acquiring Art and Antiquities

The importance of artworks' provenance documentation is uncontested.[1] All the countries should have or try to create systems that would prevent suspect or clearly illicit acquisitions of artworks.[2] Private and public collections may not plead innocence when the circumstances of artworks' acquisitions are not so clear.[3] And they are not clear when the artworks' provenance is not documented.[4]

Museums acquire artworks via purchase or donation. The application of museum ethic codes (when they have such codes) to their acquisitions reduce the number of works that the museums could and should acquire and at the same time influence the indirect acquisition of works by museums, since future donors are also influenced as far as the artworks that they are "allowed" to purchase are concerned.[5]

Certain museums, in order to contribute to the effort of tracking down artworks of unknown provenance, have also decided to publish detailed information on their collections.[6] The situation is not at all simple—it never was.[7]

In recent years there have been developed several databases of stolen art, particularly artworks looted or confiscated by the Nazis during World War II. The world's largest private database of lost and stolen art, antiques, and collectibles is the Art Loss Register.[8] Shareholders of it are, among others,[9] big auction houses, such as Christie's and Bonham's.

---

[1] Levine 2009, p. 219.
[2] Kreder 2010, p. 997.
[3] "Looting will only come to a halt when collectors refuse to purchase unprovenanced material", Lundén 2005.
[4] Kaye 2009, p. 405.
[5] "Stricter acquisition standards are necessary. Museums are established to further society's knowledge about art and culture, thus these institutions should act responsibly", see Amineddoleh 2013.
[6] Kaye 2006, pp. 255–256.
[7] Kreder 2009, p. 37.
[8] http://www.artloss.com/content/history-and-business. It seems that it has contributed to the restitution of more than 300 million dollar worth of stolen art and property.
[9] Such as insurance and art-trade industry members, see Kreder and Bauer 2011, p. 885.

E. Moustaira, *Art Collections, Private and Public: A Comparative Legal Study*,
SpringerBriefs in Law, DOI 10.1007/978-3-319-15802-0_10

There are also public bodies' databases, such as that maintained by Europe's Interpol.[10]

Certain scholars have suggested the enactment of legislation that would require museums, both public and private, to disclose information about acquisitions and to provide documents establishing good title for the artworks acquired.[11]

Beyond rules of law, beyond official law, there are the rules of social or individual ethics, the application of which may not be obligatory but is, on the other side, very important, since rules of law are or should be a minimum. It is argued that especially cultural objects' protection constitutes a moral obligation of everyone.[12]

Thus, several associations, professional or scientific, mostly private, national or international, but also international organizations such as UNESCO, have adopted Codes of Ethics or Guidelines or Recommendations that try to set the limits inside which all people involved in the circulation and protection of cultural objects should move,[13] in order for their scientific or social work to be considered as morally acceptable.[14]

The International Council of Museums (ICOM) has set forth in 1986 a Code of Ethics for Museums, which was updated in 2004 and 2006. Museums wanting to join ICOM must abide by the ICOM Code. In its recent edition, the Code calls for museums to recognize the necessity of ethical acquisition practices,[15] therefore members of the museum profession should not support the illicit traffic or market in natural and cultural property, directly or indirectly.

Thus, among several provisions of the ICOM Code of Ethics referring to those issues, it is provided that:

> Every effort must be made before acquisition to ensure that any object or specimen offered for purchase, gift, loan, bequest, or exchange has not been illegally obtained in, or exported from its country of origin or any intermediate country in which it might have been owned legally (including the museum's own country). Due diligence in this regard should establish the full history of the item since discovery or production (rule 2.3).

[10] Stolen Works of Art, INTERPOL, http://www.interpol.int/Public/WorkofArt/Default.asp.

[11] Gerstenblith 2003, pp. 462–463 has urged the enactment of such state and federal legislation.

[12] Vrellis 2011, p. 26.

[13] Among them: "Antique Tribal Art Dealers Association": Trade Practices and Guarantee, Article X, Amended Bylaws of the Antique Tribal Art Dealers Association, Inc. (1997, amended 2007); "Association of Art Museum Directors": New Report on Acquisition of Archaeological Materials and Ancient Art Issued by Association of Art Museum Directors (2008); "College Art Association": A Code of Ethics for Art Historians and Guidelines for the Professional Practice of Art History (1995); "Confédération internationale des négociants en œuvres d'art": International Support and Guidelines (1987, amended 1998 and 2005); "International Association of Dealers in Ancient Art", Code of Ethics and Practice; "Museums Association": Code of Ethics for Museums: Ethical principles for all who work or govern museums in the UK (2002); "World Archaeological Congress": First Code of Ethics (1990).

[14] Vrellis 2011, p. 26.

[15] Amineddoleh 2013.

Also:

> Museums should not acquire objects where there is reasonable cause to believe their recovery involved unauthorized or unscientific fieldwork, or intentional destruction or damage of monuments, archaeological or geological sites, or of species and natural habitats. … (rule 2.4).

And:

> Museums should abstain from purchasing or acquiring cultural objects from an occupied territory and respect fully all laws and conventions that regulate the import, export and transfer of cultural or natural materials (rule 6.4).

The ICOM Code also contains rules on the restitution by museums of cultural objects and this is extremely important.

As it was mentioned above, several (if not many) are the associations that have adopted rules or guidelines urging for due diligence when purchasing or acquiring cultural objects and for restitution to the legal owners.

Especially interesting are provisions referring to the restitution or rather repatriation of such cultural objects to indigenous communities. For example, the Museum of Anthropology (MOA) of the University of British Columbia in 1995 adopted the "Guidelines on Repatriation of Canadian First Peoples' Cultural Materials house in MOA" (revised in 2000), providing, among others:

> There are cases where it is clear that objects should be returned to a community - for example if they were illegally taken. In addition, MOA considers the return of cultural objects to individual families in cases where the objects are private and ceremonial, or left to the family under dubious circumstances.

It is not a very large-hearted provision (or, according to some other opinion, it is more realistic), though, since it is added that:

> The Museum also has, however, an interest in maintaining objects purchased with public funds in a facility accessible by the public, and in offering assistance to ensure the long-term preservation of these objects. MOA is both committed to work collaboratively with First Nations to co-manage the care and custody of cultural objects housed in MOA, and to share out museum knowledge with other museums and cultural centres.

It is observed that sometimes these ethics principles are taking a legal aspect. There are several examples of such principles in the various codes of ethics, as for example the Article 8 of the UNESCO International Code of Ethics for Dealers in Cultural Property, adopted in 1999, which provides the following:

> Violations of this Code of Ethics will be rigorously investigated by (a body to be nominated by participating dealers). A person aggrieved by the failure of a trader to adhere to the principles of this Code of Ethics may lay a complaint before that body, which shall investigate that complaint. Results of the complaint and the principles applied will be made public.

Is a specific "lex culturali*s*" created? According to an opinion, most certainly it is.[16] In any case, the rules of these codes of ethics can have a decisive role at the

[16] Vrellis 2011, pp. 40–41.

application of international conventions, when for example the application of certain provisions of those international conventions depends on the evaluation of the conduct of an involved person. They thus acquire a regulatory nature and they become a "complementary support" to the law that regulates the circulation of cultural objects.[17]

References

Amineddoleh L (2013) Museums Have a Responsibility to Protect Cultural Heritage. Aedon no 2. http://www.aedon.mulino.it/archivio/2013/2/amineddoleh.htm

Frigo M (2009) Ethical rules and codes of honor related to museum activities: a complementary support to the private international approach concerning the circulation of cultural property. Int J Cult Property 16:49

Gerstenblith P (2003) Acquisition and deacquisition of museum collections and the fiduciary obligations of museums to the public. Cardozo J Int Comp Law 11:462

Kaye LM (2006) Avoidance and resolution of cultural heritage disputes: recovery of art looted during the holocaust. Willamette J Int Law Dispute Resolut 14:243–268

Kaye LM (2009) Provenance research: litigation and the responsibility of museums. In: Nafziger JAR, Nicgorski AM (eds) Cultural heritage issues: the legacy of conquest, colonization, and commerce. Martinus Nijhoff Publishers, Leiden, pp 405–420

Kreder JA (2009) The new battleground of museum ethics and holocaust-era claims: technicalities trumping justice or responsible stewardship for the public trust? 88. Or Law Rev 88:37–93

Kreder JA (2010) The revolution in U.S. museums concerning the ethics of acquiring antiquities. Univ Miami Law Rev 64:997–1030

Kreder J A, Bauer B (2011) Protecting property rights and unleashing capital in art. Utah Law Rev 881–925

Levine JA (2009) The importance of provenance documentation in the market for ancient art and artifacts: the future of the market may depend on documenting the past. DePaul J Art Technol Intellect Property Law 19:219–233

Lundén S (2005) TV review: NRK (Norway), Skriftsamleren [The manuscript collector]. Cult Without Context 16:3–10

Vrellis S (2011) Rules of conduct in the area of cultural property. In: Samara-Krispi A (ed) Protection and return of cultural property. Sakkoulas Publications S.A., Athens, pp 25-41

[17] Frigo 2009, p. 49.

MIX
Papier aus verantwortungsvollen Quellen
Paper from responsible sources
FSC® C105338

If you have any concerns about our products,
you can contact us on
ProductSafety@springernature.com

In case Publisher is established outside the EU,
the EU authorized representative is:
Springer Nature Customer Service Center GmbH
Europaplatz 3, 69115 Heidelberg, Germany

Printed by Libri Plureos GmbH
in Hamburg, Germany